Women in Rugby

This is the first book to introduce key themes in the study of women's rugby from multidisciplinary perspectives, including history, sociology, gender studies, sport development and sport science.

Featuring contributions from leading researchers and former international players from across Canada, England, France, New Zealand and the USA, the book opens with a global history of women's rugby, locating the game in the wider context of the development of women's sport and exploring important social issues such as race, gender and violence. The book then looks at training and performance analysis at pitch level, helping the reader get a sense of the game from the ground up, before focusing on women's rugby through the eyes of others (such as rugby coaches), women's experiences of rugby's culture and promotional culture.

This is fascinating reading for anybody with an interest in women's sport, rugby, sport and social issues, sport development or sport history.

Helene Joncheray is Associate Professor at the University of Paris, France, on secondment as Researcher at the Sport, Expertise and Performance Laboratory of the French Institute of Sport (Institut National du Sport, de l'Expertise et de la Performance). She is Vice President in charge of International Relations of the International Sociology of Sport Association.

Women, Sport and Physical Activity
Edited by Elizabeth Pike, University of Hertfordshire, UK

The *Women, Sport and Physical Activity* series showcases work by leading international researchers and emerging scholars that offers new perspectives on the involvement of women in sport and physical activity. The series is interdisciplinary in scope, drawing on sociology, cultural studies, history, politics, gender studies, leisure studies, psychology, exercise science and coaching studies, and consists of two main strands: thematic volumes addressing key global issues in the study of women, sport and physical activity; and sport-specific volumes, each of which offers an overview of women's participation and leadership in a particular sport.

Available in this series:

Women's Artistic Gymnastics
Socio-cultural Perspectives
Edited by Roslyn Kerr, Natalie Barker-Ruchti, Carly Stewart and Gretchen Kerr

Women in Rugby
Edited by Helene Joncheray

For more information about this series, please visit: www.routledge.com/sport/series/WSPA

Women in Rugby

Edited by Helene Joncheray

LONDON AND NEW YORK

First published 2021
by Routledge
2 Park Square, Milton Park, Abingdon, Oxon OX14 4RN

and by Routledge
605 Third Avenue, New York, NY 10158

Routledge is an imprint of the Taylor & Francis Group, an informa business

© 2021 selection and editorial matter, Helene Joncheray; individual chapters, the contributors

The right of Helene Joncheray to be identified as the author of the editorial material, and of the authors for their individual chapters, has been asserted in accordance with sections 77 and 78 of the Copyright, Designs and Patents Act 1988.

All rights reserved. No part of this book may be reprinted or reproduced or utilised in any form or by any electronic, mechanical, or other means, now known or hereafter invented, including photocopying and recording, or in any information storage or retrieval system, without permission in writing from the publishers.

Trademark notice: Product or corporate names may be trademarks or registered trademarks, and are used only for identification and explanation without intent to infringe.

British Library Cataloguing-in-Publication Data
A catalogue record for this book is available from the British Library

Library of Congress Cataloging-in-Publication Data
Names: Joncheray, Helene, editor.
Title: Women in rugby / edited by Helene Joncheray.
Description: Abingdon, Oxon ; New York, NY : Routledge, 2021. | Series: Women, sport and physical activity | Includes bibliographical references and index.
Subjects: LCSH: Rugby football for women—Social aspects.
Classification: LCC GV945.85.S65 W66 2021 | DDC 796.333082—dc23
LC record available at https://lccn.loc.gov/2021003238

ISBN: 978-0-367-43695-7 (hbk)
ISBN: 978-1-032-04085-1 (pbk)
ISBN: 978-1-003-00554-4 (ebk)

Typeset in Times New Roman
by Apex CoVantage, LLC

Contents

List of contributors	vii
Series editor introduction	ix
ELIZABETH C.J. PIKE	
Preface	xii
DAVID COURTEIX	
Acknowledgements	xv

PART I
Women on the rugby pitch   1

1   A brief history of women in rugby union   3
    LYDIA J. FURSE

2   The development of women's rugby in the US:
    a challenging climb   15
    LAURA F. CHASE AND SARAH K. FIELDS

3   Whiteness and gendered violence on the rugby pitch   28
    ANIMA ADJEPONG

PART II
Women's rugby and performance   43

4   Training women's rugby union and sevens: not a
    simple copy-paste of men's practices   45
    ANTHONY COUDERC AND FRANCK BROCHERIE

5 Collective efficiency and performance in women's
   rugby sevens   59
   GUILLAUME SAULIÈRE, QUENTIN DELAROCHELAMBERT AND
   ADRIEN SEDEAUD

6 Evolution of social cohesion within a national rugby
   union team   74
   HELENE JONCHERAY, RENAUD LAPORTE AND PAULINE
   MAILLOT

PART III
Women's rugby through the eyes of others   89

7 The journey of a women's rugby coach: passing
   through capillarity   91
   SÉBASTIEN DALGALARRONDO

8 Women's experiences of rugby culture in Aotearoa/
   New Zealand: naked women talk about sport   101
   AMY WALLACE, STEVE JACKSON AND MARCELLE C. DAWSON

9 Beer, promotional culture and women's rugby:
   Guinness' "Liberty Fields"   116
   SARAH GEE

   Index   130

Contributors

Anima Adjepong is a postdoctoral fellow at the University of Cincinnati, USA.

Franck Brocherie is a researcher at the French Institute of Sport, France.

Laura F. Chase is a professor at California State Polytechnic University, USA.

Anthony Couderc is a sport scientist at the French Rugby Union, France.

Sébastien Dalgalarrondo is a researcher at the French National Centre for Scientific Research, France.

Marcelle C. Dawson is an associate professor at the University of Otago, New Zealand.

Quentin DeLarochelambert is a PhD student at the French Institute of Sport, France.

Sarah K. Fields is a professor at the University of Colorado Denver, USA.

Lydia J. Furse is a PhD student at De Monfort University, UK.

Sarah Gee is an associate professor at the University of Windsor, Canada.

Steve Jackson is a professor at the University of Otago, New Zealand.

Helene Joncheray is a researcher at the French Institute of Sport, France.

Renaud Laporte was an associate professor at the University of Paris-Est Créteil, France.

Pauline Maillot is an associate professor at the University of Paris, France.

Guillaume Saulière is a researcher at the French Institute of Sport, France.

Adrien Sedeaud is a researcher at the French Institute of Sport, France.

Amy Wallace was a master's student at the University of Otago, New Zealand.

Series editor introduction

The sport of rugby offers rich information to understand the development of, opportunities for and barriers to women's participation in sport, as well as potential future directions. As the editor of this book has identified, rugby has a long history of being perceived as a masculine sport for male participants and continues to be controversial as an arena for women's participation in physical activity (Joncheray & Tlili, 2013). However, rugby is also a sport that has made a significant commitment to women's equality and equity across all levels of involvement, from grass roots to high-performance participation, coaching and refereeing, governance and leadership, and visibility and fanship.

In 2017, World Rugby (the international governing body for the sport of rugby) published its Women's Development Plan with a stated ambition that:

> By 2025, rugby will be a global leader in sport, where women involved in rugby have equity on and off the field, are reflected in all strategy, plans and structures, making highly valued contributions to participation, performance, leadership and investment in the global game of rugby.
>
> (World Rugby, 2020)

This global action plan, titled "Accelerating the Global Development of Women in Rugby 2017–25," was underpinned by the "Try and Stop Us" campaign, the words of which follow.

> First rule: Try. Second rule: Try again.
> Life will hurt sometimes.
> This game will give you strength.
> To never give up, give in, or give an inch.
> Whatever your size, shape, or story.
> There's nothing you can't tackle.
> No line you can't break.

No obstacle you can't get over.
Or power straight through.
There'll be judgers, disapprovers, non-believers.
Fear less. Play more.
Because once you've started, you can't be stopped.
(www.women.rugby)

"Try and Stop Us" is a global campaign aiming to meet the strategic plan to develop women's rugby by increasing participation and engagement among fans and also attract investors in the women's game to support the objective of gender balance.

Since the launch of the campaign, participation levels among women have reached an all-time high, and approximately 40% of the global fan base is female (England Rugby, 2020). World Rugby was one of the six international sports federations to commit to the Women's Sport Leadership Academy for High Performance Coaches that commenced at the University of Hertfordshire, UK, in 2019, sending seven coaches from seven different countries. In 2020, World Rugby released its "Women Coaching Rugby Toolkit," which outlines many of the barriers to women becoming coaches, provides guidance for increasing the quantity and quality of women rugby coaches, and outlines an internship programme for coaches in the buildup to the Rugby World Cup for women in 2021.

Alongside these positive developments in women's rugby, in 2020 there was also considerable controversy following a transgender workshop held by World Rugby, which led to media reports that World Rugby was planning to ban transgender athletes from participating in women's rugby due to safety concerns (BBC, 2020). Subsequent protests accused World Rugby of flawed science and discrimination against transgender people. In particular, the discussions considered biological sex in contrast to the social aspects of gender and how an individual identifies, and they raised debates regarding the binary nature of classifying people into one of two categories of either male or female with the subsequent consequences.

These events illustrate the complexities in the development of women's sport, and specifically women's rugby, which are examined in this book. The book starts by exploring how women came to be on the rugby pitch. Lydia Furse walks us through a review of global historical developments, from the early days of women's rugby through to its inclusion in the Olympics, while Laura Chase and Sarah Fields provide a case study of developments in the USA with reference to the wider gender equality movement. Anima Adjepong then offers personal insights into gender and race issues that have impacted on the involvement of women in the sport of rugby globally. In the next section of the book, the authors consider a range of factors that influence women's performance when competing in rugby. This includes Anthony Couderc and Franck Brocherie's analysis of physiological factors that are specific to female participants; Guillaume Saulière, Quentin DeLarochelambert and Adrien Sedeaud's insights into rugby as a collective sport and the relationships and interactions between players that contribute to team performance; and Helene Joncheray, Renaud Laporte and Pauline Maillot's evaluation of the importance of cohesion in women's rugby. The final section of the book considers the wider culture of the sport of rugby from the experiences of participants, coaches and fans. Sébastien Dalgalarrondo provides fascinating insights from the perspective of a male coach of a female rugby team and his changing attitudes towards women and women's sport. Amy Wallace, Steve Jackson and Marcelle Dawson examine the culture of rugby in New Zealand amidst several scandals, the experiences of women in the sport, and the relevance to gender relations and future considerations for gender equality. Finally, Sarah Gee evaluates the lived experiences of women rugby players in the context of advertising and the commercialised relationship of women, sport and alcohol.

I am delighted that this book is published in the Routledge *Women, Sport and Physical Activity* series. In keeping with the "Try and Stop Us" campaign, it "powers straight through" the complexities that continue to surround women's involvement and progress in sport, and it delivers fascinating, informative, firsthand insights into the fast-changing world of women's rugby.

Elizabeth C.J. Pike

References

BBC (2020). *World Rugby Could Ban Transgender Women Because of Safety Reasons*. www.bbc.co.uk/sport/rugby-union/53476972 [Accessed September 19, 2020].

England Rugby (2020). *World Rugby Launch Women's Campaign.* www.englandrugby.com/news/article/world-rugby-launch-womens-campaign [Accessed September 19, 2020].

Joncheray, H., & Tlili, H. (2013). Are there still social barriers to women's rugby? *Sport in Society*, 16(6), 772–788.

World Rugby (2020). *Accelerating the Global Development of Women in Rugby 2017–25*. www.world.rugby/womens-rugby/development-plan?lang=en [Accessed September 19, 2020].

Preface

Women in rugby!

This title itself suggests expectations and projections that refer each of us to our own personality, our representations of this sport and the people practising it. These expectations themselves are indicative of the complexity and diversity of our personal, cultural and social positioning. How do women live in or on the edge of this "haven of masculinity," this sport that has become over time a symbol of virility, this microcosm long reserved for males constituting the so-called stronger sex? The theme and the variety of analyses offered arouse curiosity and fuel questioning.

My reading obviously cannot be dissociated from the special relationship I have with this sport. I have been fully engaged in rugby for a long time: as a player, an educator and then, very early on, a coach. I like its complexity, its pedagogical and educational potential, its hardness, even its rusticity and its own culture. My current position confirms and strengthens my sensitivity to the diversity of its identities, depending on the territories, countries and teams practising it. To me, rugby remains a game, like "cops and robbers" or "cat and mouse," a game for clever, cunning, intelligent and courageous people, each in their own way and each with their own personality, morphotype and physical capabilities. This is why, to me, this sport magnifies difference by emphasising the absolute richness that variety brings to a group when its members are ready to take action together.

What relationship can this multifaceted sport, with all intonations and all colours, have with gender?

Rugby, with its strong masculine connotation, constitutes a particularly rich subject of study to tackle the gender issue. Beyond this, a window examining male-female relations is opened. No, rugby is not monopolised by sex or gender.

This collection of articles provokes readers as much as the subject itself. Step by step, the authors give us an insight into this slow, gradual evolution. They identify and explain the causes while resolutely placing themselves within the framework of a changing society. They also highlight the persistent weight of representations and of a specific culture that rugby, "a men's sport," has built up over the course of its history, itself inscribed inside another history, that of the surrounding world. The authors adventurously explore the dark sides this magnificent combat sport occasionally touches, leading to some inexcusable excesses and unacceptable transgressions. However, this work also notes physiological differences, gendered this time, as if to emphasise how central they are in building performance equality on the field, verified today by the objectivity of statistics. The many approaches and the diversity of articles question, disturb, revolt, rejoice, reassure and surprise, but above all, in my eyes, underline the absolute necessity of a multidisciplinary approach when it comes to developing a performance project.

All over the world, rugby is rooted within the history of every place where it settles, flourishes and develops. A team's game style underlines its own culture and identity. There are no significant gender differences in this area. These specific features apply to both women and men without any distinction.

French women as well as French men play this game based on movement and initiative, fed by the construction of benchmarks that facilitate collective adaptability. Long forged by René Deleplace's method and his many disciples, principles and strategies continue to develop, making French teams, all genders considered, aces of the game in disorder.

There is only one notable observation on the international circuit: the absence of high-level women's teams in some major rugby countries, as a reminder that, in some places of the world more than in others, rugby remains a sport reserved for men. Statistics are clear today. With equal physical strength, volume and training conditions, female practice is identical to male practice. In a few years of professionalism in rugby sevens, females have reduced the differences that separated them from males in the frequency and intensity of runs, number of contacts, accelerations, decelerations, match activity demands, and physical, technical and mental requirements. Those differences were mainly related to the number of practice hours, which were much less numerous for women upstream, sometimes even in high-level practice. More trainable than men due to their sometimes smaller muscle mass, women build up sessions with enthusiasm and relevance. They are gradually making up for the late start in rugby culture that some of them face because of late beginnings, mostly related to social prohibitions. As a result, their passion is often exacerbated and their commitment frequently increased, which delights men invested with them on a daily basis. Convinced from the start or later, a majority of men say they are happy to share their passion for rugby with women. I totally agree.

xiv *Preface*

Daily training is of course structured exactly the same as that of males, and performance is based on the same keys. The atmosphere, climate of collaboration and group dynamics are obviously identical.

Training takes into account all the elements mentioned previously and that will be largely developed in this work.

The blossoming needs to continue in the changing, performing world of rugby that seems to be on the right track. This book, beyond its immense richness, will contribute to this awareness.

Thank you to the authors for this contribution and this production and especially to Helene for the confidence she placed in me for the writing of this preface.

David Courteix
*Head coach of the France Women's
Rugby Sevens team*

Acknowledgements

I would like to thank Elizabeth Pike for her confidence as the editor of this Routledge series *Women, Sport and Physical Activity*.

I would also like to thank the reviewers, who by their expertise have improved the book: Julien Fuchs (Université de Bretagne Occidentale), Christine Hanon (Fédération Française d'Athlétisme), Yannick Le Hénaff (Université de Rouen), Maxime Luiggi (Université d'Aix-Marseille), Richard Pringle (Monash University), Rémi Richard (Université de Montpellier) and Alexis Tadié (Université Paris Sorbonne).

Part I
Women on the rugby pitch

1 A brief history of women in rugby union

Lydia J. Furse

The recent inclusion of both men's and women's rugby sevens at the 2016 Rio Olympics represents an extent of gender parity within rugby union football, yet historically women and girls have been excluded from participating in the sport. Rugby union has traditionally been understood as a masculine-coded sport. Women have challenged the association between rugby and masculinity since the 1880s, at moments that have coincided with wider social and cultural shifts in the gender order. Through playing rugby, women in New Zealand, Great Britain and France questioned the socially imposed limitations on women's lives. In the 1880s, the 1920s and again in the 1970s, women playing rugby raised issues of gender performance, medical advisability and respectability. By the 1970s, socioeconomic conditions in many Western countries created opportunities for female participants to establish women's rugby as a sport through regional and then national governing bodies, leading swiftly to international competitions.

Despite the rich history of women playing rugby union in the late nineteenth and early twentieth centuries, there is no clear lineage between these geographically diverse events and the women's game as known today. Recorded examples of folk football in Europe since the Middle Ages indicate that both women and men took part in the premodern version of rugby (McDevitt, 2008; Porter, 2012). As rugby became codified and popularised within elite male private schools in the mid-1800s, the sport began to cultivate the ideology of rugby as a "male preserve" (Sheard & Dunning, 1973). The masculine overtone of rugby limited women and girls' access to the game for most of the nineteenth and twentieth centuries. This chapter provides an overview of the earliest known examples of women's rugby. However, there may be more women and girls who participated in rugby football whose experiences have not been privileged by the annals of history. Historians must be critical of a desire to identify "firsts" or to establish an origin for the contemporary game of women's rugby.

Although it continues to surprise the public, there are several examples of women taking up the oval ball before 1970, and with each attempt women challenged the naturalised association between masculinity and rugby. Seminal texts on the history of women's sport regularly indicate that in the late nineteenth and early twentieth centuries, the limits of acceptability excluded female participation in contact team sports such as football and rugby (McCrone, 1988; Vertinsky, 1992; Hargreaves, 1994). Yet recent research into nearly all the football codes (association football or soccer, rugby union, rugby league, American football, Aussie rules football) reveals that women, as both players and spectators, have used male-dominated team sports as a site to test gender boundaries since the 1880s (Haines, 2016; Hess, 2011; Williams, 2007; Taylor et al., 2019). Women playing rugby questioned assumptions about women's physical capabilities and their roles in the social order. Female rugby players faced significant social and cultural barriers that initially prevented the establishment of women's rugby as a competitive sport. The late-nineteenth- and early-twentieth-century transnational cases of women playing rugby football are examples that need to be understood within the sociocultural contexts that permitted some women, for short periods of time, onto the rugby pitch.

The history of women's rugby can be understood as two distinct phases, marked by 1970 as a watershed year. In the first period, women had limited access to rugby, and female participation had limited social acceptability. Public curiosity at women transgressing traditional gender boundaries encouraged sports promoters to use women's rugby as a sporting spectacle at events that could be further legitimised with charitable fundraising aims. Despite diverse examples of women playing rugby before 1970, rugby football remained a masculine-coded activity. Women's increased engagement in rugby union after 1970, as part of the wider women's sports revolution, can be considered an attempt to recode rugby union football as gender-neutral. Competitive women's rugby has developed within different national contexts from 1970 to the present day, which shaped the support or criticism female rugby players received, and are too diverse to meaningfully cover within the present study. Instead, this chapter serves as a brief introduction to the history of women in rugby union before 1970, bringing together existing literature and original primary research to highlight the different sociocultural contexts in which women negotiated access to the rugby pitch.

The first women playing rugby

A foundation story has gained traction within the world of women's rugby union, centred around the actions of a young Emily Valentine in 1887. First reported in 2010, she has emerged as the semi-official first lady of rugby. Yet the key characteristics, which are inherently critiques, of sports foundation myths as identified by Tony Collins (2011) can be applied to the Valentine story: she played a minor role in the wider development of the sport; the evidence for her involvement comes from personal affirmation with no publicly available corroborating evidence; and her story was unearthed at a particularly decisive time for the history of women's rugby, when a nineteenth century origin for women playing rugby could increase the sport's prestige. The early examples of women playing rugby football are more indicative of rugby football's perception as a masculine activity than the foundation of the women's game. Nevertheless, these examples provide insight into the unique social and cultural contexts in which some women were able to experience the joys of picking up the ball and running with it.

Playing rugby made a significant impression on the ten-year-old Emily Valentine. She recalled in her memoirs, composed almost 50 years later, the day, hampered as she was by petticoats and thick undergarments, she made it onto the pitch:

> It was just a school scratch match and they were one "man" short. I was about ten years old. I plagued them to let me play, "Oh, all right, come on then". Off with my overcoat and hat – I always wore boys' boots anyhow, so that was all right.
>
> I knew the rules. At last my chance came. I got the ball – I can still feel the damp leather and the smell of it, and see the tag of lacing at the opening. I grasped it and ran, dodging, darting, but I was so keen to score that try that I did not pass it, perhaps when I should; I still raced on, I could see the boy coming towards me; I dodged, yes I could, and breathless, with my heart thumping, my knees shaking a bit, I ran. Yes, I had done it, one last spurt and I touched down, right on the line. I had scored my try.
>
> (Exhibition, 2010; Collins, 2015, p. 374)

Despite the distance at which she wrote, Valentine recalled the strongly embodied memory in vivid detail. Although she does not mention playing rugby regularly in her memoirs, John Birch has suggested that correspondence in 1951 and other records at the Portora Royal School in Enniskillen, Northern Ireland, refer to her playing in multiple games, with Valentine siblings sometimes making up the entire back line (Birch, 2010). Victoria Dawson has described her as "the ideal 'first.'" As a middle-class child whose individual daring mirrors rugby's popular foundation myth of William Webb Ellis at Rugby School, Valentine embodies rugby union's values and is "the ideal image from which to legitimise modern women playing the game" (2017, p. 67). However, her experience did not precipitate an increase in female participation. Emily Valentine seized her opportunity to play rugby alongside her brothers, crossing the boundary from sideline to pitch.

In the same year Emily reportedly picked up the ball and ran with it, two full teams took to the pitch in Hull to play women's rugby. The game on April 8, 1887, which happened to be Good Friday, featured two teams of female players in front of a public audience at the East End club on Holderness Road, Hull. Very little is known about the Good Friday game or the players themselves. At the time, one particularly belligerent commentator, "Full Back," expressed his disgust at women playing rugby on the local men's pitch in the *Hull Daily Mail*. Despite approving of the busy rugby football schedule for the Easter weekend, "Full Back" criticised the women's game for being held on the Christian holy day, and called for the "football-loving public of Hull to withhold their support for a match that will only tend to bring the noble game into disrepute" (1887, p. 2). However, the reaction of the crowd who gathered to watch the women's exploits was memorable enough to be make the news once again, 21 years later. The spectators did not appear to appreciate the women's efforts, invading the pitch before the match was over (Anon, 1908). The Good Friday match's location in the north of England has impacted the game's historical interpretation. The game holds the ambiguous title of the first recorded women's rugby football match, rather than specifically a women's rugby union or women's rugby league match. Rugby divided into two separate codes in what has become known as the Great Split of 1895 over the issue of professionalism, with rugby league allowing players to be paid whilst rugby union maintained strict amateur regulations. Rugby league has strong links to Northern English towns and cities, and historians seeking early examples of women's rugby union may have previously dismissed the Good Friday match in Hull as an example of the rival code, despite the game occurring eight years before the Great Split. Although historians such as Dawson (2017) and Collins (2011) are rightly wary of identifying "firsts," the women of Hull deserve their exploits to be considered as the earliest recorded example of a women's rugby game.

The Good Friday game of 1887 indicates a desire by women to participate in the sporting activities of their male peers. In Auckland, New Zealand, where rugby union was fast establishing itself as the national sport, Mrs. Nita Webbe advertised for interested women to form a rugby football team in June 1891. Her plan was to commission a touring women's rugby team to play demonstration matches not only in New Zealand but across Australia and other British colonies. Webbe intended to use rugby as a commercial venture building on the popularity of rugby as a male sport and the transgressive nature of female rugby players. Her advert stated: "Wanted, 20 Young Ladies (with parent's consent) to PRACTISE FOOTBALL, preparatory to playing Auckland Ladies.- Apply, with photos" (*Otago Daily Times*, 1891, p. 3). In nineteenth-century New Zealand, the term football most commonly referred to rugby union football, rather than association football (soccer). The advert was reprinted in various newspapers across New Zealand, even as far south as Otago, over a 1,000 kilometres from Auckland. The notice suggests that the Auckland Ladies team may already have formed. According to the *Auckland Star*, the "novel scheme" featured a group of "enterprising damsels [who] practise regularly in the large building at the corner of Wellington and Pitt-streets and elsewhere, and have already obtained a fair degree of proficiency in manipulating the leather" (1891, p. 8). Nita Webbe successfully found at least some young ladies who were willing to play rugby, perhaps enticed by the offer of travel expenses and a wage of 10 shillings per week whilst on tour (*Observer*, 1891). However, the women never played a public game.

Nita Webbe designed her business venture based on public curiosity at a female sporting spectacle. Although the *Tuapeka Times* (1891, p. 2) claimed that "public opinion and hostility of the Press were strong enough to kill the abominable conception," as Webbe's scheme was a commercial venture built on the perception of female rugby players as transgressive, the press was likely to have contributed to public interest rather than have caused the abandonment of the scheme. In fact, the coverage was not entirely adverse, with several reporters indicating a degree of curiosity. Although the proposed tour did receive negative press, Webbe's intention to form two teams to tour New Zealand and Australia playing one another in exhibition matches indicates that Webbe was not attempting to develop women's rugby as a competitive sport, and the tour may have been called off because of unrelated financial reasons. Jennifer Curtin's (2017) detailed research reveals that Nita Webbe's husband faced legal difficulties in the summer of 1891, coinciding with the tour's cancellation. Given their personal circumstances, the tour's financial risk may have caused the Webbes to disband the women's rugby teams before the first match took place. Whilst the venture certainly provoked debate about the propriety of women playing rugby, particularly as a sporting spectacle for a paying audience, the social barriers may not have been the reason the tour failed. Even without playing a game, Nita Webbe's band of "enterprising damsels" challenged the societal norms that prevented women from stepping onto the rugby pitch.

The 1891 attempt to form a travelling exhibition of women's rugby, with potential financial rewards for the manageress from the gate receipts, links Webbe's scheme to the Good Friday game in Hull in 1887 and to the British Ladies Football Club, who played 20 association football matches in

1895 and whose exploits Jean Williams also described as commercially motivated rather than uniquely female-sport driven (2003). Ultimately, these nineteenth-century examples of women playing traditionally male sports did not develop women's football or women's rugby as participation activities. Instead, these ventures built on public curiosity at seeing women performing in male team sports, thereby creating a sporting spectacle. The failure of these pioneering ventures to become sustainable indicates that both rugby and football in Great Britain and New Zealand remained codified as masculine spheres in the 1880s and 1890s. Whilst Emily Valentine enjoyed an individual success in a singular instance, as did perhaps other women and girls whose rugby playing exploits have not been recorded, for the majority of women in the late nineteenth century their presence on the sidelines was tolerated, but there was no such tolerance for women's participation on the pitch.

Women playing rugby in the early twentieth century

The Great War initiated significant social changes for many women, creating opportunities for some on the rugby pitch. The prevailing middle-class norms of femininity prevented most women from playing rugby during the nineteenth century, but the First World War, between 1914 and 1918, disrupted the Victorian gender order. The loss of young men within urban communities created spaces not only in the factories but also on the pitch. Increased female participation in the traditionally masculine football codes occurred in Australia, New Zealand and Great Britain (Haines, 2016). In both employment and leisure, the First World War allowed women to fulfil traditionally masculine roles. However, women's sporting endeavours continued to primarily serve as spectator attractions, therefore representing a continuation of the nineteenth-century meaning of female participation in rugby union.

Women's rugby games undertaken for a good cause, often fundraising for war-related charities, received relatively positive coverage in the contemporary press. In New Zealand, a women's match was one of the headline attractions of the Greymouth Carnival in August 1915, from which all proceeds went to the sick and wounded soldiers fund (*Grey River Argus*, 1915; Akers et al., 2015). Equally, when female munitions factory workers formed teams to play rugby in South Wales, they received almost unanimously positive press. On September 29, 1917, thousands of spectators reportedly enjoyed a "wonderful display of scrimmaging, running, passing, and kicking" by the Newport munitions factory teams at Cardiff Arms Park. The referee, Mr. R. Pollock, stated that "he had refereed many a worse game between male teams" (Anon, 1917, p. 15). The Newport players competed in exhibition matches around South Wales, inspiring the creation of other local teams. On December 15, 1917, Cardiff Ladies faced Newport Ladies at the Cardiff Arms Park, with the visitors winning 6–0. The feat was recorded in the frame of the Cardiff Ladies team photograph, which has been preserved in the collection of the Cardiff rugby club (Prescott, 2019). The Newport Ladies rugby team successfully entered the local sporting space because their matches raised impressive gate receipts, which were donated to charitable causes. The games' charitable aims overrode concerns of appropriately gendered behaviour.

Women playing rugby could also fulfil the local desire for spectator sport. During the Great War, women's rugby appears in areas where rugby was a popular male pastime, notably Wales and New Zealand. In England, where association football was the most popular team spectator sport, female munitions workers formed football teams, such as the famous Dick, Kerr Ladies. However, women could only occupy the gender-segregated public sporting space during the war. Crowds of rugby fans were willing to see empty pitches filled by female players while traditional sportsmen were away fighting, but the support for female players vanished after the armistice. Maria Eley, who as a young woman played on the Cardiff Ladies team, recalled at the age of 106: "We loved it. It was such fun with us all playing together on the pitch, but we had to stop when the men came back from the war, which was a shame. Such great fun we had" (Prescott, 2019). For the Welsh women, a gender-segregated playing space was integral to their rugby playing opportunities. The condemnation of an attempt to form a women's rugby team in Wellington, New Zealand, in 1921 and 1922 suggests that female participation in rugby union was not socially acceptable after the war (*Evening Star*, 1922). Local desire for rugby as a sporting spectacle could be fulfilled by female players during the war, but women's rugby could not compete with men's rugby.

Sex-segregated spaces supported female participation in rugby union. In France, a women-orientated sporting space offered opportunities for women to play a version of rugby throughout the 1920s. Dr. Marie Houdré and André Theuriet adapted rugby rules to create barrette, moving the game into a female sporting space rather than women invading a male-coded playing space. Houdré popularised barrette at Femina Sport, where she was both president and barrette team captain. Femina Sport, a women's sports club based at the Stade Elisabeth, catered to middle-class Parisians, offering members sporting opportunities in a variety of activities, from athletics, gymnastics and calisthenics to netball, association football and barrette. Interest in barrette developed gradually starting in 1923, with new teams initially forming in Paris and spreading to other areas of France. By 1928, barrette was contested in both a Parisian and a national championship.

Barrette is exceptional as an example of female participation in traditionally male team sports during the early twentieth century for its relative longevity and successful defiance of bans. In 1923, the French Rugby Federation (FFR) banned male rugby clubs from hosting barrette matches. The ban used wording similar to the Football Association (FA) decree against women's association football in England in December 1921 and was similar to the way the New South Wales Rugby League blocked ladies rugby league teams from accessing sporting spaces in Sydney, Australia, in September 1921 (Michallat, 2007; Haines, 2016; Carle & Nauright, 2013). However, women continued to play barrette until the early 1930s, using predominantly women-controlled sporting spaces, which were not subject to FFR rulings. The availability of female-dominated sporting space was integral to the success of barrette during the 1920s.

Barrette, as a feminised version of rugby, radically changed the meaning of female participation in rugby union. Women were able to access competitive rugby playing opportunities, rather than just exhibition or fundraising matches. Barrette players and supporters defended their sport from critics in the sporting press by emphasising the law adaptations that differentiated it from rugby football. The 12-a-side game used a slightly smaller pitch than a standard rugby union pitch, but it still involved fast-paced running, tackles around the waist and scrummaging. As a feminised version of rugby, supporters advertised barrette as a game specifically designed to suit female participants and therefore as socially acceptable (Furse, 2019; Michallat, 2007). However, barrette attracted mixed reactions within the media throughout the 1920s, and match reports become markedly less frequent after 1930. The drop coincides with a decreased economic freedom for the middle-class women's sports clubs that had provided a specifically female space for barrette. The economic depression in Western countries during the 1930s also ushered in an era of increased social conservativism. Reinforcement of gender norms that valorised female domesticity not only impacted women in the workplace but effectively curtailed women's leisure activities. In this climate, middle-class values redefined women playing competitive barrette as intolerably unfeminine.

Barrette was a deliberate attempt to feminise rugby football, and as such it changed the meaning of female participation. Supporters used the idea that barrette had been specifically designed for women to justify female participation in a game that used skills normally reserved for male team sports, namely, contact. Barrette players denied any transgression because they were playing a sport adapted for women. The players also justified their sporting endeavours by referring to the 1920s feminist ideals of physical emancipation. However, as the 1930s ushered in a period of increasing fiscal and social conservatism, women playing a physical contact sport became totally unacceptable. The Vichy regime reinforced barrette's demise through a series of official bans in 1941 and 1942, which also banned other competitive or physically demanding women's sports (Furse, 2019). Despite barrette's relative success, the sport declined in popularity during the 1930s and disappeared entirely after the Vichy bans, with no known links between the women who played in the 1920s and the renaissance of modern women's rugby in France in 1965.

The renaissance

Women playing rugby for charitable aims was founded on the principle of public curiosity into a gender-transgressive activity, but women purposefully playing rugby for their own enjoyment can be viewed as an attempt to recode rugby football as a gender-neutral activity. In the 1960s, charitable aims provided an initial impetus for women to (re)engage as participants in rugby football. French college and university students decided to raise money for the UNICEF campaign against world hunger by playing women's rugby union matches, charging entry fees and gaining bar profits from the renowned "third half," the post-match socials. Between 1965 and 1968, women's rugby in France developed organically from the enjoyment of players thriving on spontaneous and unstructured games (Chubilleau, 2007). The growth encouraged Annie Bannier to organise the first meeting of French women's rugby team administrators, leading to the formation of the French Association of Women's Rugby (AFRF) in Toulouse on October 25, 1969. The ARFR marked a more serious and competitive structure for women's rugby in France, radically changing the meaning of female participation from a casual, spectator-focused fundraising activity to a participant-led competition. The AFRF initially had 12 affiliated teams; by 1971, it represented 330 players and 70 administrators (Chubilleau, 2007). The first national championship took place in the 1971–1972 season, with Lyon-Villeurbanne taking home the title in front of around 5,000 spectators. Although the AFRF constituted a radically different meaning for women playing rugby, prioritising competitive sport over the sporting spectacle, women's participation in rugby union football continued to face numerous social barriers (Joncheray & Tlili, 2013). But the development of competitions, organised by a national association on the eve of 1970, marked a dramatic shift in the history of women playing rugby football.

Conclusion

The fragmentary history explored here, although pioneering, does not constitute an origin of the modern, competitive game. Each new attempt by women to play rugby union arose independently, with no evidence to suggest causality or links between them. The "birth" of women's rugby, if such an event can be considered possible, is not to be found in the actions of the Hull women, or Nita Webbe's teams, or Emily Valentine. These pioneers participated in the game earlier than other female participants, but their stories cannot be conflated with foundational heroines. The impermanent nature of women's rugby before 1970 mirrors patterns identified in other women's football codes. Teams formed, played once or a handful of games, and then dissolved into historical oblivion before new pioneers restarted the cycle, never knowing of their predecessors. Even barrette, a specific reformulation of rugby football's rules to create a female-specific sport, eventually folded and left no impression upon those who later pioneered modern women's rugby in France. Future research must deepen the current perception of these events and place them in the context of other women's sports and changes in wider social history in order to understand the significant ways in which women challenged the gender order through sport, including rugby union.

Historically, the perceived relationship between rugby and masculinity severely limited women's and girls' participation in the game. The earliest examples of women participating in women's rugby matches, as opposed to individual female participants in men's or boy's rugby, unsuccessfully sought to promote women's rugby as a sporting spectacle. These ventures relied on public interest in women participating in a gender-transgressive activity, but the mixed press reactions and, in the case of the Good Friday game, pitch invasion demonstrated that it was not socially acceptable for women to participate in rugby union during the nineteenth century. The different circumstances brought about by the First World War allowed women to negotiate entry to the rugby pitch with greater ease, although still in a limited fashion. Women's rugby became an acceptable sporting spectacle, but not a competitive participation sport. Women's rugby teams formed and dissolved during the first quarter of the twentieth century as women used different techniques to negotiate a separate playing space, and despite some notable successes in South Wales and France, the impermanence of women's rugby during this period indicates the continued association between rugby and masculinity. Women's rugby has now officially been embraced by World Rugby, and women's sevens has been included in the relaunch of rugby at the Olympics starting in 2016, yet certain sporting spheres and public forums continue to view women playing rugby as a transgression of the traditional gender order. The work to redefine rugby as a gender-neutral activity is ongoing.

This chapter has provided a brief introduction to the history of women in rugby union before 1970, exploring examples from Britain, France and New Zealand. Significantly, the pioneering illustrations considered in this chapter are drawn from countries within the traditional men's rugby world. The development of women's rugby on a global scale at the end of the twentieth century offered opportunities for new participants to adopt rugby without the sport's masculine overtones. To understand the complex global development of women's rugby union will require further analysis by sociologists and historians, to which Laura Chase and Sarah Fields' chapter in this volume is a notable contribution.

References

Akers, C., Anderson, B., & Cooke, P. (2015). *Balls, Bullets and Boots*. Palmerston North: New Zealand Rugby Museum.
Anon (1891, June 2). *Auckland Star*, p. 8.
Anon (1891, June 4). Advertisements. *Otago Daily Times*, p. 3.
Anon (1891, June 13). *Observer*, p. 12.
Anon (1891, July 18). *Tuapeka Times*, p. 2.
Anon (1908, October 1). *Hull Daily Mail*, p. 6.
Anon (1915, August 26). *Grey River Argus*, p. 5.
Anon (1917, October 2). Girl footballers play at Cardiff. *Western Mail*, p. 15.
Anon (1922, April 5). Ladies at rugby. *Evening Star*, p. 5.
Birch, J. (2010). The remarkable Emily Valentine. *Scrumqueens*. www.scrumqueens.com/blogs/anonymous/remarkable-emily-valentine [Accessed November 10, 2018].
Carle, A., & Nauright, J. (2013). A man's game? Women playing rugby union in Australia. In T.J.L. Chandler & J. Nauright (eds.), *Making the Rugby World: Race, Gender and Commerce*. London: Routledge, pp. 55–73.
Chubilleau, B. (2007). *La Grande histoire du rugby au féminin*. Périgueux: La Lauze.
Collins, T. (2011). The invention of sporting tradition: National myths, imperial pasts and the origins of Australian rules football. In S. Wagg (ed.), *Myths and Milestones in the History of Sport*. New York: Palgrave Macmillan, pp. 8–31.
Collins, T. (2015). *The Oval World: A Global History of Rugby*. London: Bloomsbury.
Curtin, J. (2017). 'Before the 'Black Ferns': Tracing the beginnings of women's rugby in New Zealand. *The International Journal of the History of Sport*, 33(17), 2071–2085.
Dawson, V. (2017). *Women and Rugby League: Gender, Class and Community in the North of England, 1880–1970*. De Montfort University: s.n.
Exhibition (2010). *Extract from the Memoirs of Emily Galwey*. [Art]. Museum of World Rugby, Twickenham, England.
"Full Back" (1887, April 6). *Hull Daily Mail*, p. 2.
Furse, L. (2019). Barrette: Le Rugby Féminin in 1920s France. *The International Journal of the History of Sport*, 36(11), 941–958.
Haines, K. (2016). The 1921 peak and turning point in women's football history: An Australasian, cross-code perspective. *International Journal of the History of Sport*, 33(8), 828–846.

Hargreaves, J. (1994). *Sporting Females: Critical Issues in the History and Sociology of Women's Sport*. London: Routledge.

Hess, R. (2011). Playing with 'patriotic fire': Women and football in the antipodes during the great war. *International Journal of the History of Sport*, 28(10), 1388–1408.

Joncheray, H., & Tlili, H. (2013). Are there still social barriers to women's rugby? *Sport in Society*, 16(6), 772–788.

McCrone, K. (1988). *Sport and the Physical Emancipation of English Women, 1870–1914*. London: Routledge.

McDevitt, P.F. (2008). *May the Best Man Win: Sport, Masculinity, and Nationalism in Great Britain and the Empire, 1880–1935*. Basingstoke: Palgrave Macmillan.

Michallat, W. (2007). Terrain De Lutte: Women's football and feminism in "les Annees folles." *French Cultural Studies*, 18(3), 259–276.

Porter, L. (2012). *Shrovetide Football and the Ashbourne Game*. s.l.: Landmark Publishing.

Prescott, G. (2019). *The Earliest Photograph of a Women's Team?* [Digital Archive]. Cardiff Rugby Museum. https://cardiffrugbymuseum.org/articles/earliest-photograph-women%E2%80%99s-team [Accessed April 28, 2019].

Sheard, K., & Dunning, E. (1973). The rugby club as a type of male-preserve: Some sociological notes. *International Review of Sport Sociology*, 5(3), 5–24.

Taylor, K., Linden, A.D., & Antunovic, D. (2019). From beach Nymph to gridiron Amazon: Media coverage of women in American football, 1934–1979. *Communication & Sport*. https://doi.org/10.1177/2167479519871961 [Accessed April 15, 2019].

Vertinsky, P. (1992). *The Eternally Wounded Woman: Women, Doctors and Exercise in the Late Nineteenth Century*. Chicago: University of Illinois Press.

Williams, J. (2003). *A Game for Rough Girls? A History of Women's Football in Britain*. London: Routledge.

Williams, J. (2007). *A Beautiful Game: International Perspectives on Women's Football*. Oxford: Berg.

2 The development of women's rugby in the US
A challenging climb

Laura F. Chase and Sarah K. Fields

Rugby, for both men and women, has struggled to gain a foothold in the United States since the creation of the sport. Basketball, baseball, American football and ice hockey are generally considered to be the four most popular team sports in the country, with rugby not even making the list of top ten sports in terms of TV ratings (Das, 2020). Women in the United States have made inroads in traditionally male sports, such as rugby, American football and ice hockey, but have struggled for full acceptance in all of them. While rugby has grown at the collegiate and club levels for female rugby players in the United States over the last five decades, it has never been able to achieve National Collegiate Athletic Association (NCAA) championship sport status. In 2002, it was added to the list of emerging sports by the NCAA, often considered the fast track to NCAA championship status. However, fewer than 20 schools have fully committed to women's rugby after almost 20 years on the list. Even with several extensions of its emerging status to buy more time, women's rugby still falls woefully short of the 40-team requirement (Gewirtz, 2019).

Despite the lack of media coverage and limited popularity of rugby in the United States, US women have had some success competing at the international level. The US women's rugby team won the very first Women's Rugby World Cup in 1991 but finished only fifth in the debut of women's Olympic rugby in Rio de Janeiro in 2016. As other countries, where rugby is a major sport, have started to grow the sport of women's rugby, the US women have been losing ground. Since the inception of the World Cup for women's rugby, the United States has finished no lower than seventh, but after their strong start, the women have not finished with a medal since 1998.

Academic scholars have, over the past 30 years, examined the culture of women's rugby through qualitative and primarily ethnographic studies (Wheatley, 1994; Wright & Clarke, 1999; Broad, 2001; Shockley, 2006; Chase, 2006; Fields & Comstock, 2008; Ezzell, 2009; Joncheray et al.,

2016; Adjepong, 2017). Most, if not all, of these studies have addressed the physicality, violence and masculinity of rugby. For example, Chase (2006) argued that the physicality of the game was something that drew women to the game and was also something that differentiated rugby from most other sports available to women. Unfortunately, none of these studies looked explicitly at how outsiders perceived the sport of women's rugby nor did they interview women who did not participate in rugby due to the physicality or violence. Regardless, many of these studies do show that the physicality and aggressive nature of rugby contributed to the construction of the game as inappropriate for women, and it negatively impacts the game's popularity.

In this chapter, we will examine other factors that have hindered the development and growth of women's rugby within the United States. We will focus primarily on its status in the country as a collegiate sport and on the national print media coverage of women's rugby. Drawing upon the academic literature, print media coverage and archival materials, we explore the development of women's rugby in the United States over the past 50 years. After an exploration of the history of women's rugby in the United States, we examine the failure to achieve NCAA championship status and the quality and quantity of media coverage of women's rugby. Further, we argue that without significant changes to overcome these challenges, women's rugby in the United States will continue to underachieve.

A brief history of women's rugby in the United States

Like most sports, rugby in the United States began with the men, with the women on the margins. College men, largely in the Ivy League, had teams that played by a combination of rules from today's sports of American football, soccer and rugby. Eventually in 1868, the McGill University men's team played Harvard University in a game with rugby-union-like rules in front of spectators who paid about 50 cents each ('The History of Rugby at Yale, n.d.). Early efforts to organise the sport of rugby seem to have occurred: the *New York Times* in 1926 reported an attempt to start the International Ladies' Professional Rugby and Hockey League in about six US and Canadian cities (Women's Hockey Launched, 1926), but no further reference to this fledgling league was found. Organised women's rugby would take much longer to develop than it took with men.

The women's game in both the United States and the world really began to take off in 1968, after the first documented women's club match was held in France (Feliciano, 2016). The Portland (Maine) Women's Rugby Football Club was formed in 1969 (Portland WRFC) with enough teams following that the first United States women's rugby national championship was held in Chicago in 1978; the Portland team won (Larkin, 1978). Women's rugby championships in the United States have been held every year since 1978. The earliest teams seemed to be organised by community (such as the Portland and Chicago area teams) and by university (such as the Florida State University team founded in 1975), often with the two mixing – locals who were not students played on college club sides and students played on community sides. The sport saw growth in the early years. The southeastern region of the United States saw particularly quick growth in the mid-1970s, expanding to about 15 teams by 1980 (Shockley, 2006). Even US celebrities played: astronaut Sally Ride, the first US woman to go into space, played rugby, among other sports, while a student at Stanford University (Stevens, 1982).

Despite growth, getting official notice from the organising body of US rugby also took time. USA Rugby, founded in 1975 under a different name, fielded the first men's national team in 1976. Although an invitation-only women's team formed and toured France and England in 1985, the women's national team would not be officially organised until 1987 (About USA Rugby, n.d.). The *New York Times* reported on that 1985 European tour and gave a brief history of the sport. The article noted that in the decade since women's teams had first begun appearing in the United States, by 1985 over 250 teams with 6,000 players were in the game. US players mentioned their enjoyment of hitting and how seriously they took training while bemoaning the lack of support, as most took vacation time and paid out of pocket for the trip. At least one British player felt the Americans were talented but added, "they take the game a bit seriously for my tastes" (Grand tour for rugby team, 1985). In 1987, the US team began playing the Canadian national team, and the two continued to play against each other regularly (Da Costa, 1993).

The growth of women's rugby was not a consistent upward arc, nor was its history well-documented in the United States. Data from newspapers were often unsourced so their accuracy was unreliable, and participation rates varied by source and changed annually. A 1990 *New York Times* article noted that the governing body (then called United States of America Rugby Football Union) had 150 women's clubs with about 3,500 participants (Wallace, 1990). This was about half of what the paper had reported five years earlier, which might reflect inaccurate data, or it could reflect some changes in regional enthusiasm. Shockley (2006) traced a decline in the number of women's teams in the 1980s in the southeast region of the country and attributed it to increased opportunities in other sports, as well as some decreases in university funding because of the need to share funding with those other sports. Shockley (2006) also tied the decline to the cultural backlash in the 1980s against feminism and the rise, particularly in the south, of a conservative culture.

Women's rugby's organisation at the international level really began in the 1990s, and generally, the US women did well. In 1990, the World Rugby Festival for Women (RugbyFest) was held in Christchurch, New Zealand. It seems to have been the first international tournament of its sort, and in the final game of the two-week tournament, the US women's team lost to New Zealand (Feliciano, 2016). The next year the first Women's Rugby World Cup was held in Cardiff, Wales. A lack of sponsorship was a concern, but the organisers moved forward with 12 teams despite a last-minute legal threat from the International Rugby Football Board (IRFB), which had declined to support or to even sanction the event and then took issue with the trophy logo (Fairall, 1991).

In the 2000s, the World Cup continued but US women's dominance began to wane. After winning the first World Cup and coming in second in the next two, the US women would not make the semifinals again until 2017 when the team came in fourth. They would, though, be competitive, never finishing lower than seventh (of 16 teams) and usually finishing fifth of the standard 12 teams. Teams from New Zealand and England, countries with strong rugby traditions, have won all of the World Cups since the United States won the first one.

Because of its relative youth as a sport and its position on the edge of US consciousness, the usual national sporting bodies have not coordinated rugby. This coordination vacuum has long been an issue in tracking youth (pre-high-school sport) sport participation, but it pervades rugby at all levels. High-school sports are generally run by state high-school athletic associations under the broad umbrella of the National Federation of State High School Associations (NFHS). Some state high-school federations have, in the last few years, added rugby as a sanctioned sport, but the NFHS has not yet gotten involved. Similarly, the NCAA coordinates most US college sports, but it has not organised college championships for rugby. In 2002, the NCAA did designate women's rugby as an emerging sport, and approximately 20 women's varsity programmes at colleges participate under the NCAA's National Intercollegiate Rugby Association (NIRA). Women in these programmes are eligible for scholarships under NCAA rules, and in 2014 roughly 100 women had college rugby scholarships (Crouse, 2014). The National Small College Rugby Organization (NSCRO) was founded in 2007 and works independently of NIRA; it coordinates an estimated 40% of all US collegiate rugby.

Outside of NIRA and NSCRO, much of women's rugby has been coordinated by the national governing body of the sport, what is now called USA Rugby. In the early 1980s, women's rugby was largely regionally organised, but as the sport grew, USA Rugby's involvement in the coordination of the game did as well. In roughly 1990, USA Rugby split the women's league into a collegiate league and a club league (Champions, n.d.). Today women's club teams can compete in one of four different divisions within USA Rugby with the highest level being the Women's Premier League, which was founded in 2009. College women's teams have three different divisions in which they can compete.

Women's rugby in the United States has seen modest growth since its origins in the 1970s. Roughly 100 women's collegiate teams were registered to play in the NSCRO in 2019, and USA Rugby reported an even larger number registered with them that year. In 2010, the IRB estimated that over 20,000 females in the US were registered rugby players, which is more female ruggers than any other of the top ten rugby-playing countries (Chadwick et al., 2010). Prior to the COVID-19 pandemic, things looked bright on the national team level as well: the US women's team had qualified for the 2021 World Cup, and the first full-time coach of the women's national team was hired in 2018 (USA Taking the Long View, 2019). The women's sevens team qualified for the 2020 Olympics (since postponed) and won the HSBC World Rugby Women's Sevens Series finale in 2019 to conclude their best season in recent history (Price, 2019).

NCAA emerging status in collegiate rugby

The NCAA coordinates the majority of US collegiate sports; in many ways the organisation influences what the public considers as established or mainstream sports. Men's collegiate rugby remains outside the purview of the NCAA, but women's collegiate rugby has edged in closer primarily due to the impact of Title IX and the emerging status granted to women's rugby. Title IX requires that a school has a history of expanding women's sporting opportunities; has evidence of meeting their students' athletic interests; or has a proportional number of female athletes to full-time female undergraduates. Because most colleges started out with more men's programmes than women's, they have had to add women's sports opportunities to comply with Title IX. To achieve proportionality can be difficult at schools with American football programmes – an almost exclusively male sport at the college level (Fields, 2005). Women's rugby offers a potentially large roster with a relatively low budget, which can be attractive to schools seeking to achieve proportionality.

To provide a path to NCAA championship status in a sport, the NCAA created the emerging sports for women list in 1994. One benchmark for attaining NCAA championship status is getting 40 varsity programmes at colleges and universities within ten years (Gewirtz, 2019). In 2002, the

15-a-side version of rugby was added to the NCAA emerging sport list, but growth would be neither quick nor smooth. The first NCAA sanctioned women's rugby match was not held until Eastern Illinois University and West Chester University played in 2007 (Dohmann, 2007). In 2008 the NCAA gave women's rugby an extension of the ten-year limit to reach the 40-team benchmark. As noted previously, the NIRA was still about 20 teams short of the magic number of 40 needed to convince the NCAA to move the sport to championship status (A Case for Rugby, 2019). In 2020, the NCAA had two other sports on the emerging sport list: equestrian and triathlon. Equestrian has been on the emerging sport list since 1998 and still only has 22 varsity teams across the country (National Collegiate Equestrian Association History, n.d.), while triathlon joined the list in 2014 and has 33 varsity teams (USA Triathlon, NCAA Varsity Programs, n.d.). Rugby, like equestrian, will probably be allowed to remain on the emerging list despite the ten-year clock, but triathlon will likely be the next NCAA championship sport for women.

NCAA championship status would provide a boost for women's rugby, as it has for women's beach volleyball. However, given that women's rugby sevens is now an Olympic sport, the NCAA boost might not be as necessary. The question is whether colleges will try to offer women's sevens to capitalise on interest generated from the Olympic Games. However, from a Title IX perspective, the sevens game does not offer the same benefits to the college as the full 15-a-side game. Either way, a determined group of women's rugby advocates continues to fight to get the NCAA to recognise rugby as a championship sport.

Mediated representations of women's rugby

Women's rugby in the United States has demonstrated modest growth despite minimal mainstream or national media coverage of the game, with most coverage occurring at a local level. Most women in the United States are accessing the game at the university or club level. Unsurprisingly, a review of media newspaper coverage of women's rugby in the United States found that the vast majority of coverage has focused on collegiate or university women's rugby. The coverage of the women's national team has been very limited. It is difficult to get an exact number when so many sources are possible, but based on ProQuest searches focusing on women's rugby, approximately 80% of media coverage focused on women's university or college teams. Almost all of this coverage was provided by university or collegiate newspapers, with a very small amount of coverage of collegiate or university teams appearing in local newspapers. The *Valley News* (White

River Junction, Vermont), *Yakima Herald-Republic* (Yakima, Washington) and the *Portland Press Herald* (Portland, Maine) are all examples of local or regional newspapers that have provided some coverage of their nearby women's collegiate or university rugby teams. Many of these articles focused on reporting on specific games, highlighting individual star players, reporting on the playoff or overall season success of a team or providing an introduction to the game of rugby.

A review of national-level print media coverage revealed very little coverage of women's rugby overall compared to university, college or local newspapers. But of all the coverage of women's rugby in national print media, the *New York Times* had by far the most coverage of women's rugby. This is likely due, at least in part, to the fact that New York City was an active site for women's rugby in the late 1970s. As such, it is not surprising that the *New York Times* included articles documenting the first women's rugby game in the area and published the results of rugby tournaments in the New York City area. Thirteen articles in the *New York Times* focused, at least in part, on women's rugby between 1977 and 2016. The *New York Times*' coverage of women's rugby games began with one article published in 1977 and two articles published in 1978. The 1977 article, written by former professional golfer Jane Blalock, talked very briefly about rugby as part of the growth in women's contact sports. Harvin's 1978 article succinctly discussed the first women's 15s rugby game in the New York City area, and it detailed some of the reasons why women's rugby had been reserved for men only and one woman's efforts to promote the game. The second 1978 article explored the development of the Hartford Wild Roses women's rugby team and explained the game of rugby to an audience that knew very little about the game of rugby. Aside from a four-sentence article published in 1979 (Maine Women Win N.Y. Rugby Classic), no additional articles on women's rugby were published in the next seven years, despite the increases in participation in women's sports during this period.

A shift from a focus on only local or college rugby happened in 1985, when for the first time a *New York Times* article highlighted an international competition for US women (Grand Tour for Rugby Team). A selection of the best US women's rugby players, or what might be considered the first women's "national" team, traveled to Europe for two weeks of competition. The team went 10–0 against much weaker European opponents. The article suggested that the success of the team was due to the lack of interest in rugby in the United States, allowing women to play the game under the radar, and the lack of support for women's rugby internationally. These early successes led to the US women winning the first ever World Cup for women's rugby in 1991.

Upon examination of the national newspaper coverage of women's rugby in the United States, numerous dominant themes appeared. The pattern of the *New York Times* publishing one article on women's rugby every five to seven years continued over the next four decades. There were also clear patterns in how rugby and women's participation in rugby were portrayed in the majority of these articles. Certain central themes consistently appeared in the representation of rugby in the United States: (1) the lack of knowledge about and interest in rugby in the country; (2) the physicality of the game, especially the full-contact hitting; (3) the uniqueness of women's rugby having the same rules as men's rugby; (4) the reasons why women play the "rough" game and the importance of fun; (5) the perceived inappropriateness of rugby for women, including parents' often negative responses to their daughters playing rugby; (6) spotlight interviews of successful female players; and (7) the bawdy or party nature of rugby.

Many of the articles in the *New York Times* that focused on women's rugby began with an explanation of basics of the game of rugby or a history of the game (Harvin, 1978; Keese, 1978; Wallace, 1990; Vecsey, 2009; Fuchs, 2001). Rugby was often compared to the game of American football, imparting a very simplistic understanding of rugby. However, the differences between the two games were also emphasised in several articles. Rugby does not allow forward passing, does allow for kicking in the flow of the game, has a more continuous flow of play, allows minimal player substitutions, and has two 40-minute halves, among other differences.

The lack of understanding and exposure to rugby in the United States also meant that women's rugby was able to develop more quickly than it did in countries where rugby was an established and popular sport played by men. This rather quick development can be seen to directly contribute to the early success of the US women's national team. It was stated in 1985 that "U.S. women's rugby has developed more maybe because it doesn't have to deal with the super macho image it has elsewhere" (Grand Tour for Rugby Team). Another major factor that allowed women's rugby to develop more quickly in the United States was the political, social and legal changes of the 1970s. Title IX, passed in 1972, prohibited sex discrimination in federally funded educational institutions. As a result, the opportunities for women in sport increased dramatically in the 1970s and 1980s. The women's or feminist movement more broadly in the United States also contributed to opening doors to women in sport. "Women's rugby seems to have flourished in the United States in part because sex-defined roles have broken down there more quickly" (Grand Tour for Rugby Team, 1985).

The physicality of the game was addressed in almost every article that included some discussion of the nature of the game of rugby (Harvin, 1978; Keese, 1978; Grand Tour for Rugby Team, 1985; Wallace, 1990; Wilogren,

1999; Women's Rugby Surges, Especially on Campus, 2010; Fuchs, 2001). In "Women Taking on a Rough Challenge," William Wallace (1990) began by calling rugby one of the roughest and most demanding sports and questioned why women would want to participate in such a mean sport. Fortunately, he eventually interviewed women who played the game about their motivations for participating in rugby. The women talked about the physical and intellectual demands of the game and the diversity of skills required and downplayed the centrality of the beer keg to the game of rugby. The complexity of the game along with the physical and mental demands of the game was addressed in several *New York Times* articles, but it was central in Wallace's 1990 article. The rugby women he interviewed said, "There is a physical and mental challenge in rugby unlike any other sport" and "There are so many different components to the game it requires a lot of skills." The complexity and physicality of the game were two of the most common reasons cited for playing rugby, along with the fun of the game.

Another aspect of women's rugby that was highlighted in the media coverage of the game is that women and men play by exactly the same rules. There are only a few team sports where women and men play by exactly the same rules. This was one aspect of rugby that women playing the game thought was critical. "It's important to let women play a full-contact sport with the same rules as men . . . we have the ability to play as physically as men" (Longman, 1995). The gendering of sports has often resulted in women's games being constructed as inferior to men's games and in an overall devaluing of women's versions of games. Female rugby players in the United States considered it imperative that they were playing the same version of the game as the men because they were just as capable of playing it.

Longman's (1995) article, "As Parents Squirm, Women Happily Scrum," addressed parents' distress or discomfort with their daughters playing rugby. One parent said, "I thought she had lost her mind"; another said, "There goes 13 years of ballet lessons down the drain"; and a third said, "I don't mind a little contact, but there's $240,000 worth of dental work out there." There were also some examples of parental support for their daughters participating in rugby. Fuchs (2001) talked about one player who realised that her father loved the fact that she was playing a full-contact sport. "On the first play, she tackled someone hard, then immediately looked toward her father, whose face was lit up. 'He was saying,' Ms. Foti recalled, 'that was the football player I never had.'"

As women's rugby has grown, many of these themes have continued to be central to the construction of women's rugby, but there has also been some evolution of these themes. The growth of the game at the collegiate and university level in the United States (Women's Rugby Surges, Especially on

Campus, 2010), the growing popularity of the sevens version of the game, the return of rugby to the Olympics (Stoney, 2011, 2016), rugby's status as an emerging sport in the NCAA and the lack of resources for women's rugby in the United States have all received some coverage (Richards, 2010).

The media coverage of women's rugby in many ways mirrors the media coverage of women's sport more broadly in the United States. Overall, the quantity of media coverage of all women's sport in the country is dwarfed by the coverage of men's sport. The overall increase in media coverage of sport over the past few decades has not resulted in an increased percentage of coverage of women's sport but rather a decrease in overall percentage (Musto et al., 2017). The quality of that media coverage has also changed over time. Cooky et al. (2015) have published several articles focused not just on the amount of coverage but the quality of that coverage over a 25-year span. Increasingly, the focus has shifted from sexualised coverage of female athletes to female athletes as mothers, or it presents female athletic performance as uninteresting or lackluster (Cooky et al., 2015). The overall message we get is that women's sport is not as important as men's sport and that women's roles as mothers devalue their athletic accomplishments. The even fewer media representations of women's rugby continue to suggest that participation in the game is not something a typical female would want to do. Those who play are represented as being a little bit different simply because they play.

Future/conclusions

US women have been playing organised rugby for about half a century, but the game has not grown in proportion to the growth of other women's sports. Rugby has remained on the precipice of becoming a popular sport for women in the United States, with seemingly insurmountable obstacles in its way. The barriers to growth in women's rugby, even beyond the Olympic delay, are many and complex, without easy solutions, and they have existed since the beginning of the women's game in the 1970s. The lack of media attention on women's rugby in the United States has hurt the game both because of a lack of awareness of its existence and because of the representation of the game and the females who play it. Historically, articles about the game have been few and far between, and although they are often somewhat positive, noting the success of individuals or teams and noting the camaraderie, they often tell the same basic story. With only one article every five years or so, the newspapers may feel comfortable repeating that story, but it does not help the game grow or suggest that the game is mainstream enough for traditional sports reporting. Representation of the sport as an oddity keeps it relegated to that status.

Unlike in other more rugby-centric countries, most US women are first exposed to the game at the collegiate level, having had no previous experience of the game. On the one hand, this suggests that the lesser known game of rugby in the United States is not constructed in the same masculine light as it is in countries with strong rugby traditions. This fact at times seems to have opened the door, especially in the 1980s and 1990s, to women's participation in small numbers. Few in the United States noticed; therefore, few cared enough to oppose women's participation. On the other hand, no one plays a sport they have never heard of, and without a strong rugby tradition, the various organisations must create the structure for the development and growth of the game from the earliest youth teams through the elite national teams.

The organisational structure of women's rugby has been and remains diffuse and somewhat nebulous. A strong youth base is needed for the sport to achieve the participation numbers necessary to be granted full NCAA championship status and to help the game grow at more elite levels. USA Rugby, however, has not been the strong, consistent and financially solid organising body that some might have hoped for. Instead, local and state high-school-level sports organisations have begun to fill the organisational void. NCAA-affiliated groups and colleges and universities have worked on smaller levels and so offer minimal to moderate support of local teams. This diffuse organisation might, though, protect the game while USA Rugby struggles financially, as other organisations may be poised to step in and provide direction and opportunities.

Despite these vast challenges, women's rugby in the United States has managed to hang on and, in fact, to grow over the last 50 years. While the growth has not been as swift or as steady as its supporters might desire, the players and the game get credit for carrying on. This suggests a kind of resiliency among those who love and support the game, a trait that will help them to persist and to make it continue to grow in a postpandemic world. Those in the game have an opportunity to reshape the representation of the game with social media, reorganise the game with the decline of the traditional organising bodies, rethink ways to increase the safety of the game, and reevaluate how to financially support it all. Women's rugby is a tough game on many levels, but that toughness in the players and supporters portends a brighter future.

References

About USA Rugby (n.d.). *USA Rugby*. www.usa.rugby/about-usa-rugby/ [Accessed February 12, 2020].

Adjepong, A. (2017). 'We're, like, a cute rugby team': How whiteness and heterosexuality shape women's sense of belonging in rugby. *International Review for the Sociology of Sport*, 52(2), 209–222.

Blalock, J. (1977, July 1). Women and their future in sports: More muscle, more contact games. *New York Times*, p. S2.

Broad, K.L. (2001). The gendered unapologetic: Queer resistance in women's sport. *Sociology of Sport Journal*, 18(2), 181–204.

A Case for Rugby (2019). *NIRA Rugby*. https://soundcloud.com/user- 915715876/a case-for-rugby-ncaa-emerging-sports-forum-12519 [Accessed February 12, 2020].

Chadwick, S., Semens, A, Schwarz, E.C., & Zhang, D. (2010, March). *Economic Impact Report on Global Rugby Part III: Strategic and Emerging Markets*. https://web.archive.org/web/20110626220118/www.irb.com/mm/Document/NewsMedia/MediaZone/02/04/22/88/2042288_PDF.pdf [Accessed February 12, 2020].

Champions (n.d.). *USA Rugby*. www.usa.rugby/club/championships/ [Accessed February 12, 2020].

Chase, L.F. (2006). (Un)disciplined bodies: A Foucauldian analysis of women's rugby. *Sociology of Sport Journal*, 26(2), 109–120.

Cooky, C., Messner, M., & Musto, M. (2015). 'It's dude time!': A quarter century of excluding women's sports in televised news and highlight shows. *Communication and Sport*, 3(3), 261–287.

Crouse, K. (2014, May 22). Need scholarship? Join scrum. *New York Times*, p. B11.

Da Costa, N. (1993, June 9). Women's rugby: Canada closing gap on US. *Ottawa Citizen*, p. C6.

Das, S. (2020, January 21). Top 10 most popular sports in America 2020 (TV ratings). https://sportsshow.net/most-popular-sports-in-america [Accessed February 12, 2020].

Dohmann, G. (2007, September 12). Women's rugby set for NCAA debut. *USA Today*, p. 10C.

Ezzell, M. (2009). 'Barbie dolls' on the pitch: Identity work, defensive othering, and inequality in women's rugby. *Social Problems*, 56(1), 111–131.

Fairall, B. (1991, April 6). Rugby union. *The Independent* (London), p. 47.

Feliciano, J. (2016, March 22). History of women in rugby. *National Small College Rugby Association*. www.nscro.org/news_article/show/628281 [Accessed February 12, 2020].

Fields, S.K. (2005). *Female Gladiators: Gender, Law, and Contact Sport in America*. Champaign: University of Illinois Press.

Fields, S.K., & Comstock, R.D. (2008). Why American women play rugby. *Women in Sport and Physical Activity Journal*, 17(2), 8–16.

Fuchs, M. (2001, November 4). The rugby mystique. *New York Times*, p. WE1.

Gewirtz, J. (2019, January 16). NCAA emerging sports list at 25. *Sports Travel*. www.sportstravelmagazine.com/ncaa-emerging-sports-at-25/ [Accessed February 12, 2020].

Grand Tour for Rugby Team (1985, November 27). *New York Times*, p. B11. www.nytimes.com/1985/11/27/sports/grand-tour-for-rudby-team.html [Accessed February 12, 2020].

Harvin, A. (1978, April 17). Rugby: Women join in traditions. *New York Times*, p. C3.

The History of Rugby at Yale (n.d.). www.yalerfc.com/history [Accessed January 24, 2020].

Joncheray, H., Level, M., &, Richard, R. (2016). Identity socialization and construction within the French national rugby union women's team. *International Review for the Sociology of Sport*, 51(2), 162–177.

Keese, P. (1978, November 19). No longer on the sidelines. *New York Times*, sec. 23, p. 2.
Larkin, M. (1978, October 31). Portland wins national women's classic. *Rugby*. https://drive.google.com/file/d/0Bz25vzHyvrQuY1RuTF9BczRvT0U/view [Accessed February 12, 2020].
Longman, J. (1995, May, 8). As parents squirm, women happily scrum. *New York Times*, p. A1.
'Maine Women Win N.Y. Rugby Classic (1979, September 24). *New York Times*, p. C8.
Musto, M., Cooky, C., & Messner, M. (2017). "From fizzle to sizzle!" Televised sports news and the production of gender-bland sexism. *Gender and Society*, 31(5), 573–596.
National Collegiate Equestrian Association (n.d.). *History*. https://collegiateeques trian.com/sports/2019/4/3/_131987884234813832.aspx [Accessed February 20, 2020].
Price, K. (2019, June 16). One day after qualification, U.S. Women's rugby sevens wins first ever HSBC Sevens title. *Team USA*. www.teamusa.org/News/2019/June/16/One-Day-After-Olympic-Qualification-US-Womens-Rugby-Sevens-Wins-First-Ever-HSBC-Sevens-Title [Accessed April 30, 2020].
Richards, H. (2010, August 20). No career, but women get to butt heads, too. *New York Times*, p. B11.
Shockley, M.T. (2006). Southern women in the scrums: The emergence and decline of women's rugby in the American southeast, 1974–1980s. *Journal of Sport History*, 33(2), 127–155.
Stevens, W.K. (1982, May 2). Feminism paved astronaut's way. *New York Times*, p. 70.
Stoney, E. (2011, December 1). For women's rugby, road to Olympics starts in Dubai. *New York Times*. https://www.nytimes.com/2011/12/02/sports/rugby/02iht-rugby02.html [Accessed March 18, 2021].
Stoney, E. (2016, January 29). Where rugby is king, few seek Olympic crown. *New York Times*, p. 11.
USA Taking the Long View (2019, November 19). *USA Rugby*. www.rugbyworld cup.com/2021/news/540549?lang=en [Accessed February 12, 2020].
USA Triathlon, NCAA Varsity Programs. (n.d.). www.teamusa.org/usa-triathlon/about/multisport/ncaa-triathlon/varsity-programs [Accessed February 20, 2020].
Vecsey, G. (2009, October 11). Americans celebrate victory for rugby: Sports of the times. *New York Times*, p. SP11.
Wallace, W.N. (1990, May 22). Women taking on a rough challenge. *New York Times*, p. D27.
Wheatley, E.E. (1994). Subcultural subversions: Comparing discourses on sexuality in men's and women's rugby songs. In S. Birrell & C. Cole (eds.), *Women, Sport and Culture*. Champaign: Human Kinetics, pp. 193–211.
Wilgoren, J. (1999, December 12). What was won on the playing fields of Antioch. *New York Times*, pp. 33.
Women's Hockey Launched (1926, April 11). *New York Times*, p. S7.
Women's Rugby Surges, Especially on Campus (2010, April 17), *New York Times*. https://www.nytimes.com/2010/04/18/sports/rugby/18rugby.html. [Accessed March 18, 2021].
Wright, J., & Clarke, G. (1999). Sport, the media and the construction of compulsory heterosexuality: A case study of women's rugby union. *International Review for the Sociology of Sport*, 34(3), 227–243.

3 Whiteness and gendered violence on the rugby pitch

Anima Adjepong

It was a hot summer evening in central Texas, and I was attending rugby practice with a local team. Summer evenings in Texas are quite hot, and that August evening in 2011 was no different. With sweat dripping down our arms, hair sticking to our necks and faces and shorts brown with dirt, the 20 players on the pitch transitioned from playing touch rugby to a metabolic conditioning workout. Our task was to push a large, commercial truck tire down the length of the field in pairs. To show encouragement, players called out to one another: "Make this tire your bitch!" "Flat back; use your legs; titties out." "Good job, ladies!" These words of support provide some insight into the forms of gendered aggression and pleasure that players express on the rugby pitch. Lifting truck tires is not in and of itself an act of violence. However, the way players discussed the activity demonstrates an overall ethos of gendered violence attached to the sport.

References to violence in this chapter acknowledge both its subjective and objective forms. Subjective violence has a clear perpetrator, an agent that inflicts damage – the player that makes "this tire [her] bitch." Objective violence on the other hand is *systemic* and/or symbolic violence embedded into the social structure. Objective violence is not easy to perceive because it is the violence inherent to a supposedly nonviolent state of things (Zizek, 2008). In the case of my observations at the rugby practice, objective violence is evident in the underlying sexism apparent in the use of the term "bitch" to indicate domination. Making something or someone your bitch means dominating them. This particular mode of domination is sexist, because bitch is a derogatory word for woman. Despite the use of bitch, however, players also relished in their cisgender femininity by calling attention to using their breasts as part of their athletic efforts. Likewise, players also called one another ladies. In men's sports, calling other players ladies, bitches or pussies is a form of heterosexism and misogyny (Schacht, 1996). Yet in the context of this practice session, and in women's sports more generally, "ladies" subverted the insult and instead emphasised players' gender as women. The use of language in this way emphasised the players' gender and thus challenged feminine norms, while also paradoxically reproducing objective violence in the form of sexism. Through their language and actions, the players destabilised what it means to be a lady and an athlete and granted themselves permission to take pleasure in using their bodies to run, jump and tackle. But by employing the same sexist language as the men, they also reproduced subjective violence in the form of sexist conventions about violence and women's subordination.

Women rugby players' experiences of the sport centre on ideological contests around race, class and sexuality. Assessment of the pleasure, pride and panic that players disclose about their participation in the sport is inadequate without careful attention to how each of these social classifications animates and informs players' experiences. Whilst there is extant scholarship about gender and sexuality in studies of women's rugby (Broad, 2001; Ezzell, 2009; Hardy, 2015), a discussion of race, vis-à-vis whiteness, remains limited in the literature. Paying particular attention to whiteness provides a more complete analysis of the intimate relationship between sport and broader society. More specifically, with regard to how sport animates social change, attention to whiteness can reveal the iterative ties between forms of social privilege and resistance to inequality.

This chapter focuses on two aspects of subjective violence in rugby – tackling and the injuries that may be sustained during matches – as a means of discussing the systemic (objective) violence reproduced through the sport. I begin by providing a brief description of the social context of women's rugby in the United States. My theoretical framework articulates how intersectionality and whiteness studies inform the forthcoming analysis. I then offer a review of the scholarship on women's sports and violence, with an emphasis on rugby. After discussing my methods, I present my findings, which turn on key insights from players about how they accepted tackling as a part of the sport and shared their reflections on pleasure or panic during tackles. The subsequent discussion reveals some ambivalence about how players articulated their pleasure and pride in deploying their bodies on the rugby pitch. I conclude by drawing connections between players' descriptions of their experiences of violence and their positionality in a white, heterosexual patriarchy.

The gender and racial context of rugby in the United States

This study took place in the United States, where a disproportionate number of rugby players are white and male. In its 2019 survey of players, USA Rugby (2019) recorded that 85,000 men played compared to 30,000 women. USA Rugby does not collect data on players' race, but attend any rugby tournament and you will encounter a sea of whiteness. A lack of racial diversity, coupled with sexism, sustains the systemic violence manifest on the rugby pitch. The social context of women's rugby in the United States presents a rich site for examining how whiteness informs players' claims to pleasure and pride in enacting sporting violence (Adjepong, 2017). Taking this context into account is crucial to a complete understanding of the challenge sportswomen pose to articulations of masculinity with violence.

An intersectional look at white, heterosexual femininity

Over the years, whiteness has received increased scholarly attention as a racialised and structural position of power and privilege (Frankenberg, 1994; hooks, [1992]; Lipsitz, 2006). Whiteness is a privileged signifier that operates as the somatic norm – the body that needs no explanation when it takes up social space because it is always seen as belonging (Ahmed, 2006; hooks, [1992]; Puwar, 2004). Increasingly, sports studies have articulated the importance of paying special attention to how whiteness shapes this terrain (Long & Hylton, 2002; Scraton, 2001; Watson & Scraton, 2001, 2017). This increased attention has revealed how whiteness animates women's sport studies (Adjepong & Carrington, 2014; Bruening, 2012). Yet, an analysis of whiteness remains undertheorised. Through its focus on how whiteness informs women's rugby players' discussion of their experiences of violence, this chapter directs much needed scholarly attention to how racialisation confers special privilege to white players and facilitates the reproduction of racism and sexism.

In addition to whiteness studies, intersectionality frames the forthcoming analysis. An intersectional analysis considers how categories such as race, gender and sexuality are co-constructed (Crenshaw, 1991). Furthermore, such an analytical approach addresses the material consequences of race, gender, class, nation and sexuality and thus allows for an examination of people's individual experiences within larger social constructs. Black studies scholar Jennifer Nash (2008) calls our attention to the need to deploy intersectionality as an analytical tool for examining how "privilege and oppression can be co-constituted on the subjective level" (p. 11). This chapter offers precisely such an analysis by examining how, under heterosexism, whiteness nevertheless offers women rugby players some level of freedom.

Women's sports, enacting violence and whiteness

Advances in women's sport participation in the Western world coexist with societal pressure for sportswomen to follow norms of heterosexual femininity (Whitson, 2002). Nevertheless, in sporting contexts, women also adhere to disciplinary norms of athleticism, including using their bodies as tools that can cause others and themselves physical harm (Markula, 2003; Shogan, 1999). By taking control of their bodies on the sports field, women may challenge the idea that femininity is passive. In rugby contexts, scholars have suggested that players engage in unapologetic behaviour to affirm their place on the pitch (Chase, 2006; Ezzell, 2009; Hardy, 2015). This unapologetic stance challenges social ideas around heterosexual femininity and affirms women's right to be unruly, violent and aggressive on and off the playing field. The aforementioned scholarship demonstrates how, despite advances in women's sports, athletes' expressions of violence remain transgressive and proscribed, thereby positioning players who relish in their embodiment of strength and physicality as nonconventional women.

Despite being unapologetic about their athleticism, sportswomen nevertheless confront pressure to embody a "hetero-sexy" image. Players may be identified as too muscular or too strong and, therefore, not feminine enough (Toffoletti, 2016). In rugby, this censure remains the case even though the sport requires athletes to train their bodies to withstand the force of the sport and perform well. When women play rugby and leave the field with injuries, research has shown that these players experience marginalisation. One study in the United Kingdom found that women rugby players who had visible bruises had to navigate being identified by strangers and others as victims of interpersonal violence (Gill, 2007). Another study in France on women rugby players' injuries concluded that "people seem to find it more difficult to accept injuries when the body is a woman's rather than a man's" (Joncheray & Tlili, 2013, p. 781).

Although sportswomen face social stigma, studies demonstrate that these athletes also feel a sense of empowerment and individual agency when they challenge the social norms that stigmatise their embrace of physicality (Beaver, 2016; Hardy, 2015; Liechty et al., 2015). These players navigate a social context in which women ought to be demure, heterosexual and appealing to men. As Beaver (2016) showed in his study of roller derby players, this context presents a challenge to how players demonstrate their individual agency and resist heterosexist norms about women's athleticism and dress sense.

The studies discussed previously identify how athletes navigate social constraints about gender and sexuality. However, rarely is whiteness noted as a resource or barrier that sportswomen may draw on to challenge these constraints. Elsewhere, I have argued that whiteness enhances the freedom and empowerment with which women rugby players in the United States challenge feminine norms (Adjepong, 2016, 2017). Specifically, I showed how white, heterosexual, middle-class women possessed forms of cultural and social capital that allowed them leeway in how they challenged feminine norms (see also Beaver, 2016). Whiteness characterises how women rugby players discuss their relationship to violence in important ways. The hegemonic culture in the United States privileges white, heterosexual femininity whilst as the same time imposing strict limits on how free white women can be. This paradox is evident in sports, politics and even in the workplace (hooks, 2013; Williams, 2013). Nevertheless, whiteness remains underidentified as a factor in how women navigate the contradictions of freedom and empowerment.

Methods and positionality

The motivating goal for the study from which this chapter derives was to critically examine how women discussed their experiences in a sport sometimes described as "a hooligan's game played by gentlemen" (Collins, 2009). Interviews are a useful method for learning other people's observations and perceptions about their subjective experiences (Weiss, 1995). Responses provide insight into players' unique experiences and how they make sense of their social world. Although the study was primarily interview-based, I also conducted participant observation during the spring (2012) and summer (2011 and 2012) rugby seasons. Additionally, I reflected on and included my own history as a rugby player since 2005 to draw overall conclusions. Observations at tournaments showed me the relational ways in which women players interacted with one another, male players and match officials. It was also an opportunity to participate in rugby rituals at after-game celebrations, where I could observe how players bonded and shared the pleasure of playing with one another.

I conducted in-depth, semistructured interviews with a convenience sample of 15 women rugby players in central Texas and southern California. Twelve participants were white, two were Latina and one was Black. The youngest participant was 18 years old and the oldest was 36. All but one respondent had at least a bachelor's degree. Four interviewees reported dating men exclusively, two reported dating both men and women and the remaining nine reported dating women exclusively. Women's rugby can be what Jayne Caudwell (2002) calls a "dykescape," a space where queer sexuality can be freely expressed. As such, rugby spaces can be welcoming of sexual and gender diversity. Yet some women's rugby spaces also accommodate a staunch defence against the lesbian stereotype associated with the sport (Adjepong, 2017; Ezzell, 2009; Hardy, 2015). This aggressive stance against lesbians reinforced the glass closet by forcing queer players to denounce their sexuality in order to fully belong on their teams (Griffin, 1998).

I recruited study participants by attending rugby tournaments and contacting teams through Facebook groups and email. Interviews lasted between 30 and 90 minutes, with the average length of an interview being about 45 minutes. I conducted six interviews at tournaments, five at bars, two in people's homes, one on the telephone and one in my respondent's office. I audiorecorded and transcribed all interviews, after which I deleted the audio files. I conducted a preliminary round of open coding using ATLAS.ti qualitative data analysis software. Following the first round of coding, I combined codes as I identified themes throughout for my analysis. I then wrote memos to help me codify and make sense of the data. These memos and codes inform the subsequent analysis.

The findings that follow offer representative statements from research participants around the themes of tackling and injuries. From these statements, I provide an analysis of how ideological contests inform players' sense-making about their experiences. Throughout, I show how this discourse reflects the objective violence that normative whiteness and heterosexism register on the sporting terrain.

Tackling: ambivalence, pleasure, pride and panic

A rugby tackle is typically one-on-one and involves a player grabbing her opponent and pushing her to the ground. I asked all participants whether or not they liked tackling. Out of 15 research participants, only two were unequivocal about their love of tackling. The remaining 13 players identified some aspect of this embodied violence that they enjoyed, while expressing distaste for other parts of it. The following statement encapsulates the ambivalence players expressed about this ubiquitous aspect of playing rugby.

> I hate tackling people. Yeah, I would much rather get tackled than have to tackle somebody. . . . You're taught how to do it and that's the sport.

In this comment, the player, a 26-year-old member of the US military and recreational rugby player, articulated her ambivalence about tackling. First, she was unequivocal in her claim that she did not enjoy the act of pushing another player down with a tackle. Instead, her preference was to be the player knocked down. Yet, in her reflection that "you're taught how to do it and that's the sport," this athlete was calling attention to the expectations that come with playing rugby. The reality is that when you choose to play rugby, whether or not you like to tackle, at some point in your rugby career you are probably going to have to do it. Therefore, although she preferred to be on the receiving end of a tackle, this research participant had also accepted that she had to use her body to knock other players down in order to effectively play. All but two research participants echoed the above statement in one way or another. While this player used the strongest language – "I hate tackling" – all interview respondents expressed some trepidation about using their bodies in this way.

Although research participants expressed their dislike of tackling as demonstrated in the preceding paragraph, they also nevertheless expressed great pride in successfully executing a tackle. The following statement from a 36-year-old mathematics professor is illustrative.

> I do like tackling. Tackling feels really good, especially if it's a good tackle. There've been times when I've tackled bigger women. . . . I like when we've been practising something and we execute it, it actually goes well. Like we've actually done it well, oh that feels *so* good.

The player was about 5 feet, 2 inches tall. When she talked about tackling women bigger than herself, she was expressing pride in her ability to use her smaller body to bring others to the ground. By adding the component about successfully executing a move from practice, this player was also emphasising her pride in how, through practice, she could control her body to accomplish the difficult task of tackling. All research participants expressed the kind of pleasure described in the preceding statement in one form or another. The ability to successfully execute tackles was very important to players and legitimated their experiences as rugby players.

Similar to the preceding comments, which demonstrate pride of accomplishment, the following statement from a 26-year-old social worker illustrates the experiences of pleasure that players disclosed about using their bodies to tackle.

> Yes! Yes, I do enjoy tackling. I guess my coaches are like there's a natural instinct in me to always want to make contact with somebody. . . . I guess I'm just naturally physical and so I think that's one of the things that I really enjoyed is just the physicalness of the sport.

This statement reveals the pleasure this player felt in making contact with others through a tackle. When she said she enjoys "the physicalness of the sport," she was emphasising the pleasure of using her body in an athletic capacity. By naturalising her enjoyment of physicality, this player was also making an essentialist claim about her sporting ability. She was not alone in this articulation of "natural aggression." Ten of the 15 participants in this study described themselves as naturally aggressive and therefore ideal rugby players.

Although all interviewees expressed great pride and pleasure in their ability to tackle effectively, three others who had witnessed or experienced severe injuries also disclosed great fear about what could happen should a tackle go wrong. For example, one player, who played in the open field, expressed her concerns about tackling by telling me,

> At fullback there are quite a few times where it's just you and the other person, who has the ball. It's really terrifying when they are just running at you full speed and you're more or less just left to the will of destruction. I've hurt myself numerous times in open field tackles because there's so much energy colliding and it has to go somewhere and it comes back on me [points at herself] and you get hurt that way. . . . However when they're executed and you hit an open field tackle you feel awesome. You feel like you just conquered the world.

As this player reflected on her fears, she also noted the feeling of exhilaration that accompanies a successful open-field tackle. Although she described alarm at having another player come full speed at her and expressed concern about being hurt from the sheer force of the collision, she also emphasised the pride and pleasure in successfully using her body in this way.

The preceding quote brings together the various strands of emotions that this section has sought to present. The participants in this study revealed some ambivalence about using their bodies to tackle and force other players to the ground. This ambivalence came from contradictory concerns around getting hurt or hurting others (more on this to follow) and the feeling of successfully executing a tackle. As such, players also expressed pride and pleasure – that feeling "like you just conquered the world," which as the mathematics professor described just "feels *so* good!" The way that participants in this study described their experiences of tackling encapsulates the diverse emotions that come up when they use their bodies in ways that free them from normative expectations about femininity (Markula, 2003). The underlying fear of injury tempered the feelings of pride and pleasure that they described.

An important yet unstated aspect of the complex emotions that players disclosed about tackling emerges when we consider research participants' embodiment as white women. The rugby players in this study confronted a social landscape in which their bodies are more likely to be identified as victims and not perpetrators of violence (Adjepong, 2016). As such, the claim of "natural aggression" and pride in successfully executing tackles implicitly challenge social conventions that say that as women, they must comport themselves passively (Heywood & Dworkin, 2003). Their whiteness facilitates expressing an affinity for violence without reproducing racist stereotypes or pathologising pride. When women of colour, and in particular Black women, engage in behaviour identified as aggressive, they confront hostility. Media reports about Serena Williams' style of play as too manly, too aggressive and all wrong are examples of the way gender deviance is attributed to Black women (Adjepong & Carrington, 2014; Douglas, 2002; see also Bailey, 2016). The objective violence of this racist, heterosexist, cultural landscape informs how the white women in this study discussed their experiences of pleasure and pride in tackling.

Turning now to players' discussion of injuries, inflicted or sustained, I show how the ethos of the sport produced responses to injuries that were as ambivalent as players' responses to tackling. These responses suggest that the participants in this study understood their experiences of their bodies in context. As players of a sport that requires them to use their bodies in forceful ways, they developed a stance that minimised their fears and concerns as much as possible, while emphasising their pleasure.

Inflicting and sustaining injuries

Minor injuries, cuts and scrapes are so ubiquitous in rugby that, when I asked participants in this study if they had ever been injured, they typically responded in the negative before listing several wounds they had incurred through play. It seemed that for the interviewees, an injury had to include a fractured bone and a hospital visit to count. As one player explained, "It's just, you know, you deal with it. It's expected. . . . You're going to get hurt. It happens." Another participant, responding in the negative to the question "Have you ever been injured?" told me,

> Fortunately, no, I've never had something so bad that I was out for months and months and months. I've had, you know, like sprained shoulders that hurt for a few months, and sprained ankles, but that's about it.

For this player, sprained shoulders and ankles did not constitute injuries because they did not keep her out of the game for long periods of time. Although she disclosed that her sprained shoulder hurt for a few months after the injury occurred, she continued to play and as such did not consider the pain a real injury. Other players also mentioned mild concussions and sprains as not real injuries. In other words, sustaining a personal injury in rugby was almost unremarkable for all of my research participants. As athletes who experienced their bodies as powerful, playing through pain was expected and they took on this role with little complaint.

Just as sustaining injuries seemed to be a nonissue for all the participants in this study, inflicting injuries also seemed inconsequential. The wrong body in the wrong place was often used as an explanation for why bad injuries happened. The following quote demonstrates how players typically explained to me how bodies needed to be in the right position as a way to avoid injury. The player quoted next was about 5 feet, 6 inches tall and told me she weighed 182 pounds. As she reported,

> Don't stick me out on the wings, because that doesn't make any sense. I mean strategically, it makes no sense, because I'm going up against somebody who is maybe 140 [pounds]. If I hit her, she's going to be hurt. I'm going to hurt her. And I, I'd feel bad for like seconds. I'd do it again, but I'd feel bad for seconds.

The preceding quote suggests that the player only felt a tinge of guilt about potentially inflicting injury. By first noting the poor strategic decision of placing a player her size out on the wings, this participant pushes off responsibility for the consequences of potentially hurting another player. Despite noting the heightened risk of causing an injury by playing in the open field, the player also demonstrates her commitment to the game by saying that she would execute a tackle again even if it meant that someone got hurt.

Most of the participants in this study revealed similarly cavalier attitudes about potentially injuring other players through tackles. Such statements did not mean that players were indifferent to causing injuries. Instead, through their awareness that playing rugby could cause injuries, they developed a relaxed attitude towards this consequence. I asked all participants if they had ever injured another player. The typical response was similar to the following quote:

> Um, have I ever injured [anyone]? Yes. I think I messed up an ankle tackling her. It was 15s season in Vegas. And she was out [i.e., unable to play]. I was able to keep playing, yeah. I didn't physically . . . I mean I didn't intentionally [do it]. Like no, no, no. I'm not out for blood. So [as far as any injuries] that I know of . . . I've tackled many girls.

In this quote, the player clarified that she is aware of injuries she may have caused other players during a rugby match. However, she also asserted she did not hurt others intentionally. Instead, by noting that she had "tackled many girls," this research participant was also calling attention to the heightened possibility of unintentional injuries simply as a result of playing rugby. Consequently, although taking responsibility for any injuries she was aware of causing, the player was clear that inflicting injuries is part of the game. One must simply get used to it.

Whilst most research participants discussed inflicting injuries similarly to the players just described, one respondent shared a particularly jarring narrative about hurting another player:

> I tackled the scrumhalf [lowers voice and speaks deliberately], this really small girl. And I tackled her so hard her head hit the ground and she went into convulsions and like almost died. Yeah, it was pretty scary. She was like frothing at the mouth and like the ambulance had to come and stuff. It sounds really bad. I [weighed about] 100 more pounds than her. Not [literally] a hundred more pounds [but] she was really, really little [compared to me]. She was like, Hispanic or maybe Indian or something? A really little girl; she probably weighed like a 100 pounds soaking wet. I mean you gotta think about that when you're playing. I mean, I'm a big woman, but I have been knocked on my ass too by girls that are bigger than me.

In the retelling, it is clear that this player was affected by the injury. Lowering her voice to describe how the other player almost died reflected the seriousness of what had occurred. Yet, by also highlighting the size difference and noting that the other player had to consider the possibility that she might be so severely injured that she would need an ambulance, this player shifts the blame onto the injured player. Furthermore, by explaining that she had also been "knocked on her ass," this research participant was implicitly equating the other player's convulsions with the kind of tackles that the previous respondent described as having "tackled many girls."

There is also an overtly racialised component in the discussion of this injury. Elsewhere, I have discussed how white rugby players rhetorically produce themselves as the normative and appropriate type of rugby body, while as the same time constructing certain racialised others as athletically superior or inappropriate for the sport (Adjepong, 2017). Although other players' race did not come up in discussions of injuries and tackling, the unstated position of whiteness informed how players reported their pride, pleasure and concerns about injuries, especially their consequences off the playing field (Adjepong, 2016). The conclusion takes up this theme of whiteness to explore how players' discussions of tackling, sustaining and inflicting injuries are animated by their privileged position as (primarily) white, middle-class women.

Conclusion: objective violence and whiteness as resource

Whiteness was a resource through which players discussed their relationship to rugby and their embodied empowerment. Although mostly unstated in research participants' descriptions of their pride, pleasure and panic in executing tackles and sustaining and inflicting injuries, racialisation plays a part in how they discussed these actions. With one exception, all the players quoted earlier are white women. As white women, the participants in this study felt comfortable naturalising their aggression. Because white femininity is *a priori* constructed as in need of protection, staking a claim to a natural sense of aggression and thereby taking pride in executing tackles is a form of resistance. Whiteness also acted as a resource for players to enact a "queer unapologetic" (Broad, 2001) or claim to be "Barbie dolls on the pitch" (Ezzell, 2009). However, as noted, studies that position white women as challenging norms of femininity often discount whiteness. Perhaps this silence is due to the fact that neither researchers nor research participants often name their own whiteness (Watson & Scraton, 2017).

Rare mentions of race also highlight how whiteness operated in this study context. Interview respondents mentioned race when I asked their racial identities and on exactly two other occasions. The first occasion was when one player told me that "Samoans are good rugby stock." By this claim she was naturalising rugby ability to a racialised nonwhite other and reproducing the myth of the normal, white body (Adjepong, 2017). The second occasion was quoted earlier when the participant noted the nonwhite race of another player she injured. In these moments, the racialisation of other players magnifies the whiteness of participants who understand their experiences to be racially neutral.

The way players in this study discussed their experiences of rugby normalised the objective violence of racism and sexism associated with rugby. Despite their use of heterosexist language (e.g., "make this tire your bitch"), players also challenged sexist exclusions of women in a male-dominated sport like rugby. Their participation in the sport potentially loosened forms of gender inequality on a subjective level. But on an objective level, the social structures of sexism remained intact through players' contributions to sexist discourse. This paradox at the intersection of whiteness and gender advancement reveals how white women's experiences of gender equality can ironically sustain and reproduce the forms of violence associated with white, heterosexual patriarchy. Likewise, how whiteness shapes players' experiences of their embodied physicality as athletes reveals how processes of racialisation are produced and challenged in sport.

References

Adjepong, A. (2016). 'They are like badges of honour': Embodied respectability and women rugby players' experiences of their bruises. *Sport in Society*, 19(10), 1489–1502.

Adjepong, A. (2017). 'We're, like, a cute rugby team': How whiteness and heterosexuality shape women's sense of belonging in rugby. *International Review for the Sociology of Sport*, 52(2), 209–222.

Adjepong, A., & Carrington, B. (2014). Black female athletes as space invaders. In Hargreaves, J. & Anderson, E. (eds.), *Routledge Handbook of Sport, Gender and Sexuality*. London: Routledge, pp. 189–198.

Ahmed, S. (2006). *Queer Phenomenology: Orientations, Objects, Others*. Durham: Duke University Press.

Bailey, M. (2016). Misogynoir in medical media: On Caster Semenya and R. Kelly. *Catalyst: Feminism, Theory, Technoscience*, 2(2), 1–31.

Beaver, T.D. (2016). Roller derby uniforms: The pleasures and dilemmas of sexualized attire. *International Review for the Sociology of Sport*, 51(6), 639–657.

Broad, K.L. (2001). The gendered unapologetic: Queer resistance in women's sport. *Sociology of Sport Journal*, 18(2), 181–204.

Bruening, J.E. (2012). Gender and racial analysis in sport: Are all the women white and all the blacks men? *Quest*, 57(3), 330–349.

Caudwell, J. (2002). Women's experiences of sexuality within football contexts: A particular and located footballing epistemology. *Football Studies*, 5(1), 24–45.

Chase, L.F. (2006). (Un)disciplined bodies: A Foucauldian analysis of women's rugby. *Sociology of Sport Journal*, 26(2), 109–120.

Collins, T. (2009). *A Social History of English Rugby Union*. London: Routledge.

Crenshaw, K. (1991) "Mapping the margins: Intersectionality, identity politics, and violence against women of color". *Stanford Law Review*, 43(6), 1241–1299.

Douglas, D.D. (2002). To be young, gifted, black and female: A meditation on the cultural politics at play in representations of Venus and Serena Williams. *Sociology of Sport Online-SOSOL*, 5(2), 1–16.

Ezzell, M.B. (2009). 'Barbie dolls' on the pitch: Identity work, defensive othering, and inequality in women's rugby. *Social Problems*, 56(1), 111–131.

Frankenberg, R. (1994). *The Social Construction of Whiteness: White Women, Race Matters*. Minneapolis: University of Minnesota Press.

Gill, F. (2007). 'Violent' femininity: Women rugby players and gender negotiation. *Women's Studies International Forum*, 30(5), 416–426.

Griffin, P. (1998). *Strong Women, Deep Closets: Lesbians and Homophobia in Sport*. Champaign: Human Kinetics Publishers.

Hardy, E. (2015). The female 'apologetic' behaviour within Canadian women's rugby: Athlete perceptions and media influences. *Sport in Society*, 18(2), 155–167.

Heywood, L., & Dworkin, S.L. (2003). *Built to Win: The Female Athlete as Cultural Icon*. Minneapolis: University of Minnesota Press.

hooks, b. [1992]. Representations of whiteness in the black imagination. In *Cultural Studies*. Eds. Lawrence Grossberg et al. London: Routledge, 338–346.
hooks, b. (2013, October 28). Dig deep – beyond lean in. *The Feminist Wire*. https://thefeministwire.com/2013/10/17973/ [Accessed August 12, 2019].
Joncheray, H., & Tlili, H. (2013). Are there still social barriers to women's rugby? *Sport in Society*, 16(6), 772–788.
Liechty, T., Sveinson, K., Willfong, F. & Evans, K. (2015). 'It doesn't matter how big or small you are . . . there's a position for you': Body image among female tackle football players. *Leisure Sciences*, 37(2), 109–124.
Lipsitz, G. (2006). *The Possessive Investment in Whiteness: How White People Profit from Identity Politics*. Philadelphia: Temple University Press.
Long, J., & Hylton, K. (2002). Shades of white: An examination of whiteness in sports. *Leisure Studies*, 21, 87–103.
Markula, P. (2003). The technologies of the self: Sport, feminism, and Foucault. *Sociology of Sport Journal*, 20, 87–107.
Nash, J.C. (2008). Re-thinking intersectionality. *Feminist Review*, 89(1), 1–15.
Puwar, N. (2004). *Space Invaders: Race, Gender and Bodies Out of Place*. New York: Berg.
Schacht, S.P. (1996). Misogyny on and off the "pitch" the gendered world of male rugby players. *Gender & Society*, 10(5), 550–565.
Scraton, S. (2001). Reconceptualizing 'race', gender and sport: The contribution of Black feminism. In B. Carrington & I. McDonald (eds.), *Race, Sports and British Society*. London: Routledge, pp. 170–187.
Shogan, D. (1999). *The Making of High Performance Sport: Discipline, Diversity, and Ethics*. Toronto: Toronto University Press.
Toffoletti, K. (2016). Analyzing media representations of sportswomen – expanding the conceptual boundaries using a postfeminist sensibility. *Sociology of Sport Journal*, 33(3), 199–207.
USA Rugby. (2019). *USA Rugby Member Stats*. http://membershipstats.usa.rugby/ [Accessed August 12, 2020].
Watson, B., & Scraton, S. (2001). Confronting whiteness? Researching the leisure lives of South Asian mothers. *Journal of Gender Studies*, 10(3), 265–277.
Watson, B., & Scraton, S. (2017). Re-confronting whiteness: Ongoing challenges in sport and leisure research. In Watson, B. & Scraton, S. (eds.), *Race, Gender and Sport*. London: Routledge, pp. 85–106, edited by Beccy Watson and Sheila Scraton.
Weiss, R.S. (1995). *Learning from Strangers: The Art and Method of Qualitative Interview Studies*. New York, NY: Simon and Schuster.
Whitson, D. (2002). The embodiment of gender: Discipline, domination and empowerment. In S. Scraton & A. Flintoff (eds.), *Gender and Sport: A Reader*. London: Routledge, pp. 227–240.
Williams, C.L. (2013). The glass escalator, revisited: Gender inequality in neoliberal times, SWS feminist lecturer. *Gender & Society*, 27(5), 609–629.
Zizek, S. (2008). *Violence: Six Sideways Reflections*. New York: Picador.

Part II
Women's rugby and performance

4 Training women's rugby union and sevens
Not a simple copy-paste of men's practices

Anthony Couderc and Franck Brocherie

With the advent of professionalisation in rugby union (after the 1995 South Africa World Cup) and rugby sevens (nearly ten years later with the Rio 2016 Summer Olympics), the emergence of financial contracts and sport marketing, in addition to some changes in regulations, has contributed to make the game faster and more attractive. As such, global rugby participation involves more than 8 million registered and nonregistered players worldwide, of which 2 million are women. In France, of the 210,000 men and 22,000 women registered in rugby union, 20 men and 25 women players are professionally engaged in rugby sevens with the French rugby union federation. In addition, sports science services have grown and propose a wide array of support to optimise performance. This is potentially beneficial for the development of rugby union and sevens, in particular for women who switch from one code to the other (although possible, this is much less likely with men). For example, during the last edition of the women's rugby union World Cup played in Ireland in 2017, 31 professional rugby sevens players represented the best nations.

Alongside professionalisation, the introduction of technology such as the Global Positioning System (GPS) in team sports (e.g., football, Australian football, cricket, field hockey, netball, lacrosse) (Cummins et al., 2013) has considerably grown over the last few years and has improved the understanding of men's and women's rugby union and sevens time-motion analysis. GPS-based time-motion analysis provides some useful information about players' locomotion activities and the match's physical and physiological demands, and it could be used to monitor players' external loads. In the meantime, several epidemiological studies have been commissioned by the World Rugby governing body to study rugby-union- (Fuller et al., 2016) and sevens-related injuries (Fuller & Taylor, 2018). Important findings about women's rugby-induced injuries question the strength and conditioning approach as the best to prepare fitness and prevent injury among women players.

This chapter describes the women's rugby union and sevens match analysis and fitness performance, as well as their related injuries, in reference to men's rugby union and sevens activities. Then, evidenced-based practices and recommendations are provided for maintaining women players' homeostasis and developing their fitness level, while preventing physical injuries.

Performance analysis of women's rugby union and sevens

Women's rugby union and sevens are played similarly to their male counterparts (i.e., with the same rules, pitch size and equipment). However, despite efforts to equalise playing patterns between genders, physical and physiological inequalities still exist and require specific attention for women's rugby performance optimisation. To date, little attention has been paid to the anthropometric and physiological characteristics of women's rugby union and sevens players. Although maximal oxygen consumption (~48 ml kg^{-1} min^{-1} in rugby union, reported to be similar to elite women's football players) (Nicholas, 1997) and muscle strength are naturally lower in women compared to men (mainly due to differences in body size and composition, hormonal status, sociocultural influences and dietary habits) (Shephard, 2000), the differences in the anthropometric and physiological measurements reflect the demands of the different playing positions as generally reported for men's and women's rugby union players (Nicholas, 1997; Sheppy et al., 2020).

Regarding the metabolic response to high-intensity exercise, a lower glycolytic activity is generally reported in women (Ruby & Roberts, 1994), potentially due to a lower cross-sectional area of fast-twitch muscle fibres and/or lower glycolytic enzyme activity (Hausswirth & Le Meur, 2011). During dynamic contraction, women could be less fatigable than men during a low-load and slow-speed dynamic fatiguing task (Hunter, 2016). After multiple sprints, women exhibit less muscle fatigue than men, mainly due to lower absolute initial sprint performance (Billaut & Bishop, 2012). However, when the initial sprint is similar between genders, the difference no longer persists, indicating comparable muscle recruitment strategies to perform repeated sprints. Interestingly, even though women are also subject to muscle damage, they are able to recover more rapidly than men (Sewright et al., 2008). This is likely because they have a greater capacity for recycling adenosine triphosphate supply than men, granting them a better aptitude for the next intense, brief exercise bout. Several studies attempted to describe the divergence throughout the menstrual cycle with low levels of circulating oestrogen and progesterone in the early follicular phase affecting carbohydrate, free fatty acid and protein metabolism (Hausswirth & Le Meur, 2011).

Such menstrual cycle phase differences also potentially impact women's rugby union and sevens performance.

Match demands

To date, several studies have investigated match or tournament demands in women's rugby sevens (Suarez-Arrones et al., 2012; Portillo et al., 2014; Vescovi & Goodale, 2015; Goodale et al., 2017; Doeven et al., 2019; Malone et al., 2020; Reyneke et al., 2018; Clarke et al., 2015a, 2017). Although different time-motion approaches are used, movement patterns are generally described using variables such as total distance, relative distance (distance covered per minute), locomotor activities at low and high intensities, number of accelerations and maximal speed. According to the systematic review of Sella et al. (2019), international-level women's rugby sevens players cover an average of $1{,}623 \pm 17$ m per match, corresponding to 98 ± 12 m min^{-1}, with 12.4 ± 1.5 accelerations per match for a sprinting length averaging 3.9 ± 1.2 m and a maximal speed reached during a game of 7.3 ± 0.4 m s^{-1}. Although the total distance covered by male players (1,600–1,800 m per match) appears similar, relative distance (110–120 m min^{-1}) and maximal speed (8.5 ± 1.1 m s^{-1}) are higher (Higham et al., 2012). In this systematic review (Sella et al., 2019), the small number of studies using the same high-speed threshold do not allow a clear comparison between men's and women's rugby sevens locomotor activities. Table 4.1 summarises the data from the available studies on international women's rugby sevens.

Table 4.1 Summary of time-motion analysis studies in international women's rugby sevens

Authors	No. of subjects	No. of matches	Total distance (m)	Relative distance (m min^{-1})	Maximal speed (m s^{-1})
Suarez-Arrones et al. (2012)	12	5	$1{,}556 \pm 189$	103 ± 10	NA
Clarke et al. (2015a)	12	6	$1{,}066 \pm 89$	105 ± 5	NA
Portillo et al. (2014)	29	12	$1{,}642 \pm 171$	NA	NA
Vescovi et al. (2015)	16	18	$1{,}468 \pm 88$	95 ± 5	7.4 ± 0.5
Goodale et al. (2017)	20	30	$1{,}352 \pm 306$	87 ± 11	6.9 ± 0.8
Clarke et al. (2017)	11	12	$1{,}078 \pm 197$	86 ± 4	8.5 ± 3.9
Malone et al. (2020)	27	36	$1{,}625 \pm 132$	117 ± 9	7.5 ± 1.4
Doeven et al. (2019)	12	5	$1{,}465 \pm 432$	NA	NA

NA: not available

Data discrepancies may be due to several contextual variables (e.g., opponent playing level, tactics of the teams) as well as possible methodological bias (e.g., low number of players and/or games used).

In comparison, women's rugby union players cover, on average, 5,820±512 m per match (vs. 7,000–7,900 m for men's rugby union), corresponding to 68 m min^{-1} and a maximal speed of ~6.7 m s^{-1} during an international match (Suarez et al., 2014; Lacome et al., 2014). In the absence of consensus regarding speed thresholds to define low-intensity, high-intensity and sprinting activities, the comparison of rugby union and sevens remains hazardous. In this view, Clarke et al. (2015) and Doeven et al. (2019) compared three different speed thresholds: an absolute threshold (arbitrarily fixed by the GPS manufacturer, 5.5 m s^{-1}) and two relative thresholds corresponding to the speed of ventilatory threshold (VT; velocity associated with the ventilatory threshold (vVT2) and VT2 speed, 3.5 m s^{-1}). The results indicate that vVT2 might be preferred to define high-intensity activities for women players. It is noteworthy that the widely used threshold of 5 m s^{-1} inherited from men's rugby union and sevens likely underestimates (up to 30%) the volume of high-intensity running performed by women players. Therefore, men and women players should not be monitored with the same speed threshold during training.

According to Clarke et al. (2015a, 2017) and Doeven et al. (2019), high-intensity activities correspond to 25–36% of the total distance covered during an international women's rugby sevens match. Of note, the French women's rugby union and sevens national teams' high-intensity performance corresponds to 9% and 28%, respectively, of the total distance covered (Couderc et al., unpublished data). With rugby sevens requiring repetition of such effort up to six times over a 48- to 72-hour tournament period, this clearly highlights that women's rugby sevens players might be easily prepared to play in women's rugby union but not the opposite.

The repetition of high-intensity efforts

Contrary to common belief, rugby sevens combines frequent, high-intensity running and collisions, which may explain why its practice may prepare players well for rugby union. Beyond locomotor requirements, rugby sevens is characterised by the repetition of high-intensity effort (RHIE), which includes high-intensity runs, acceleration and collisions (Couderc et al., 2019). During a game, men's rugby sevens players performed, on average, eight high-velocity runs, nine accelerations and ten collisions, composing approximately four RHIEs (Couderc et al., 2019). In women's rugby sevens, such an analysis of RHIE has not been conducted yet. Nevertheless, seven high-velocity runs, eight accelerations and twelve collisions per female player per match are generally reported (Couderc et al., unpublished data), which does not appear to be distributed differently than men's rugby sevens players.

Such data highlight the importance of RHIE in women's rugby sevens, which may be (or not) related to the most intense periods of play (i.e., "worst-case scenario") (Sheppy et al., 2020). If this "worst-case scenario" analysis over a 60-second period differs between women's (143–161 m min^{-1}) and men's rugby union players (154–184 m min^{-1}) and holds across positions and period (60 s to 600 s) (Cunningham et al., 2018), it may facilitate the design of game-specific training programmes that better prepare players for these decisive moments of a game. Requiring players to perform such "worst-case scenario" situations that include high-intensity runs, accelerations and collisions – with more high-intensity runs and accelerations for men and more collisions for women – interspersed with short inter-effort recovery periods (< 21 s) would undoubtedly be useful to adequately prepare them for the demands of the game, while reducing their risk of sustaining an injury.

Epidemiology of women's rugby code-related injuries

Rugby union and sevens are collision sports that are associated with high injury rates, independent of gender. The World Rugby governing body has implemented injury surveillance in major rugby union and rugby sevens tournaments. Injury has been defined as

> any injury sustained during a match or training activity that prevents a player from taking a full part in all normal training activities and/or match play for more than one day following the day of injury.
>
> (Fuller et al., 2017)

Accounting

A significant number of injuries has been recorded in rugby sevens, with higher figures than those reported in rugby union. For example, compared to the men's rugby union 2015 World Cup, which reported an injury incidence of 90 per 1,000 hours of play (Fuller et al., 2017), 152 injuries per 1,000 hours of play were reported during the 2017–2018 World Sevens Series in men's rugby sevens (Fuller et al., 2018). In women's rugby sevens, the injury rate increased to 121.5 per 1,000 hours of play over the 2018–2019 season (Fuller et al., 2018). In comparison, Taylor et al. (2011) reported a match-induced injury incidence of only 3.5 per 1,000 hours with a mean severity of 55 days and median severity of nine days in women's rugby union. Most common injuries were caused by tackles, with 15%

concerning knee-ligament injuries resulting in the highest number of days lost (43%).

Because women face social pressures regarding physical appearance, a negative energy balance in women players would lead to chronic fatigue, decreased alertness and sleep disturbances, which lead to an increased protein metabolism and compromise muscle resynthesis (Hausswirth & Le Meur, 2011; Snyder, 1998). Such a state would amplify the risk of injury in rugby union and sevens. Furthermore, in addition to biomechanical (Hewett et al., 2005), neuromuscular (e.g., deficits in hamstring activation in women during dynamic neuromuscular control of the knee) (Hewett et al., 2005) and postural control differences between men and women in core stabiliser muscles and lower limbs (e.g., with greater hip adduction and internal rotation with decreased knee flexion, women are predisposed to increased knee valgus) (Imwalle et al., 2009), women are three to four times more likely to suffer anterior cruciate ligament injuries than men (Agel et al., 2005). It is noteworthy that in women players, nine out of ten injuries (vs. eight out of ten injuries in men players) (Fuller & Taylor, 2020) are related to a collision.

Injury risk factors

In rugby sevens, particular attention must be focused on strength and conditioning in order for players to be able to cope with the match demands, which are increasing with playing standards in both men and women players. Furthermore, independent of gender, it has been shown that in-play sequences increased from group stages to final stages during the World Sevens Series tournaments (Ross et al., 2014). Fatigue development over the tournament, mainly due to the accumulation of matches, likely increases the risk of injury from match to match (Fuller et al., 2016). The risk of injury is twofold higher after only two days of competition, indicating the importance of properly managing player turnover in order to maintain competitiveness and limit injury occurrence.

For example, Clarke et al. (2015b) reported substantial muscle damage (increase in creatine kinase) after two days in women's rugby sevens players participating in a tournament. This was largely attributed to the high-intensity running. Even if in the second half, the total distance covered and high-intensity activities are reduced in comparison to the first half, the number of collisions remains unchanged in men's rugby sevens (Peeters et al., 2019). This might explain the 60% higher risk of injury observed in the second half (Fuller et al., 2016; Cruz-Ferreira et al., 2018). Overall, to avoid such a scenario, reaching a high fitness level and managing men and women players (e.g., turnover, recovery process) in competition are paramount.

Strength and conditioning and injury prevention (prophylaxis)

As previously mentioned, women's rugby union and sevens have embraced professionalisation over recent years, with an increase in training volume, intensity and frequency whatever the playing standard (even if some differences persist between women's rugby sevens amateur and elite levels) (Portillo et al., 2014). With an increasing number of matches played, the level of opposition and injury risk, any rugby-related practitioner must be aware of the necessity to conduct prophylactic strength and conditioning programmes. While injury prevention is part of the men's training process, this approach is relatively new and not yet systematic for women players. Such gender-specific and individualised preventive work might first rely on the identification of injury risk profiles through fitness assessments, including straight sprint, agility, anaerobic capacity (such as repeated-sprint ability or Wales Anaerobic Test) (Beard et al., 2019), endurance capacity, functional movement screening and body composition (Jones et al., 2016). Based on these assessments, gender-specific injury prevention could be initiated from the beginning of the player's development process via (1) standard prevention sessions that could be scheduled within the preparatory period and/or (2) preventive work that could be included in daily training and integrated as a common thread of performance.

Standard injury-prevention session

Considered as a training session per se, these standard injury-prevention sessions must be identified and scheduled individually or collectively by the background staff at a frequency of one to three sessions per week. The women players themselves can devote time for this preventive approach as part of personal development concomitant to the collective training. In such a case, exercises proposed remain general and must be adaptable, at least partially, to the functional need of the women players. Of note, contrary to their stronger male counterparts, women can perform such sessions without any additional load (most often using body weight alone) unless they are able to master techniques for movement with additional weights. If women players have benefited from specific training and they are able to master techniques for movement (which is not often the case), then they should work with additional weights. Figure 4.1 illustrates a standard injury-prevention session individualised for the French women's rugby sevens national team players. In this example, exercises align with women-specific prophylaxis requirements, such as (1) ability to control the lumbopelvic region to allow optimum production, transfer and control of force

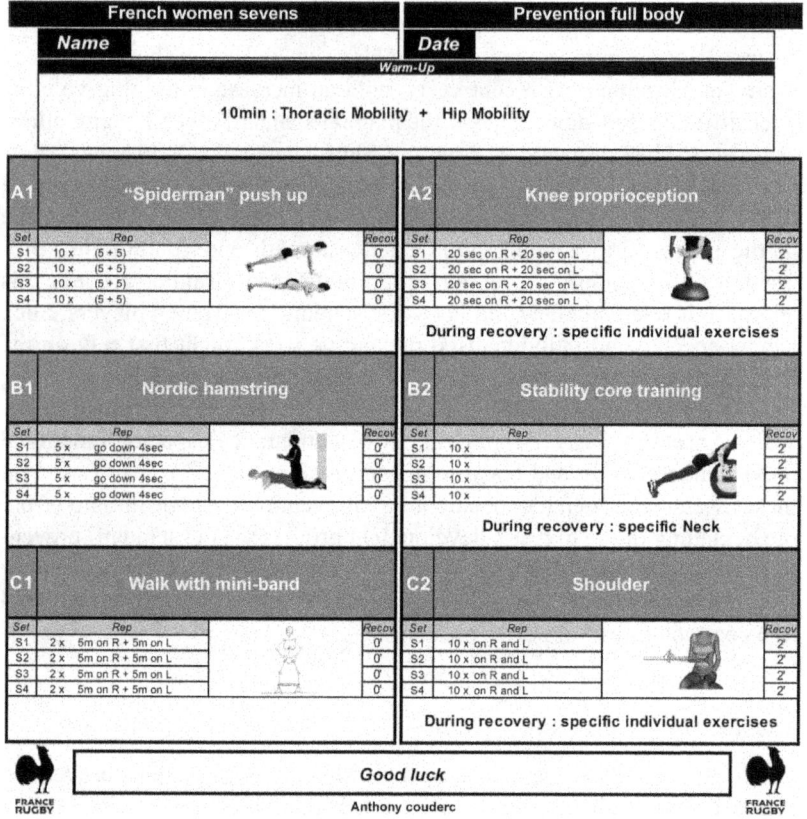

Figure 4.1 Typical standard injury-prevention session conducted with the French women's rugby sevens national team

and motion (see sequence A1–A2); (2) strength capacity of the shoulder complex (see sequence B1–B2); (3) proprioception faculty to prevent anterior cruciate ligament injury (see sequence C1–C2); and (4) integration of personalised prevention exercises.

Preventive work as a common thread

In France, the women's rugby union and sevens national teams' staffs focus on activation, which is a preparatory phase that includes mobility, stability, and muscular and nervous solicitation. Contrary to conventional warm-ups, the activation-based warm-up is not limited to an increase in

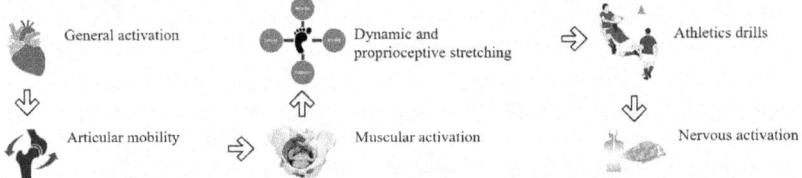

Figure 4.2 The activation-based warm-up process

cardiorespiratory activity and subsequent rise in core temperature. The activation is organised in six steps aimed at optimising performance while preventing injury occurrence. Suitable for both rugby union and sevens as well as the female gender, these steps include general activation, articular mobility, muscular activation, dynamic and proprioceptive stretching, athletic drills and nervous activation (Figure 4.2).

General activation

The physiological purpose of general activation is to increase blood flow and to elevate core and muscle temperatures. This first step, which is no longer than two minutes, is mainly based on low-intensity, locomotor activities. Its modality depends on the subsequent training content but also on players' habits and needs. Ambient temperature, time of day and whether it is the first activity of the day or not will also influence the type of activation.

Articular mobility

The second step aims to improve movement amplitude by eliminating articular constraints that are susceptible to perturb the correct execution of any skill. For this, automassage using sticks, ball or foam rolling (with different diameters) would be useful (Behara & Jacobson, 2017). Such "deep" massage might promote muscle relaxation via local vasodilation (which further increases blood flow) and reduction of fibrous tissue adhesions, thereby acting on muscle flexibility. If this "unlocking" phase primarily targets the joints that will be then solicited during training, the thoracic spine, lumbar spine, pelvis and hips are systematically mobilised.

Muscular activation

The third step focuses on stability, notably via the activation of deep core muscles (i.e., pelvic girdle, hip extensors and/or scapular girdle). In this view, the gluteus, hip adductors and abductors and core muscles are the muscles to activate with more or less volume of work. Depending on exercise selection, this step could be part of corrective intervention.

Dynamic and proprioceptive stretching

Such exercises aim to prepare the muscle for the specific constraints of the activity in terms of dynamic amplitudes, in order to improve the quality and also the control of the movement. It is worth mentioning that balance and proprioception fluctuate during the different phases of the menstrual cycle (Emami et al., 2019), thereby requiring particular attention for women.

Athletic drills

By integrating movement through athletic drills, the objective of this step is to continue the muscular activation initiated in previous steps. The introduction of technical drills (i.e., with a ball) would further increase muscle temperature and blood flow. At the same time, particular attention would be focused on execution quality, which might improve positioning, segmental alignment and intra- and inter-coordination through activation repetitions. Over time, this might result in greater stability, better running technique and higher efficiency.

Nervous activation

The final step refers to nerve stimulation in order to "switch on" the players. For that, completion of postactivation, potentiation-induced preloading can improve subsequent physical performance. The use of heavy-resistance exercises (e.g., 85% of one repetition maximum in back squats and Olympic lifts) or more practical, ballistic-style activities, such as drop jumps and weighted jumps, are suggested to improve neuromuscular activation and contractility (McGowan et al., 2015). Moreover, the use of technical drills would favour transfer to the training.

Conclusion

Alongside professionalisation, the physical demands of rugby union and sevens have increased. Despite efforts to equalise playing patterns between men and women, physical and physiological inequalities still exist and require specific attention for women's rugby performance optimisation and injury prevention. For that, appropriate training intervention (with a particular focus on repeated high-intensity exercises and/or "worst-case scenario") and programming (ideally taking the menstrual cycle into account) are crucial for women players' performance and health. Bearing in mind the physical and physiological gender differences, strength and conditioning coaches should apply evidence-based interventions with a particular focus on the individualisation of activation and prevention sessions within the overall training process.

References

Agel, J., Arendt, E.A., & Bershadsky, B. (2005). Anterior cruciate ligament injury in National Collegiate Athletic Association basketball and soccer: A 13-year review. *The American Journal of Sports Medicine*, 33(4), 524–531.

Beard, A., Ashby, J., Chambers, R., Millet, G.P., & Brocherie, F. (2019). Wales anaerobic test: Reliability and fitness profiles of international rugby union players. *Journal of Strength and Conditioning Research*. doi: 10.1519/JSC.0000000000003448. [Online ahead of print].

Behara, B., & Jacobson, B.H. (2017). Acute effects of deep tissue foam rolling and dynamic stretching on muscular strength, power, and flexibility in division I linemen. *The Journal of Strength & Conditioning Research*, 31(4), 888–892.

Billaut, F., & Bishop, D.J. (2012). Mechanical work accounts for sex differences in fatigue during repeated sprints. *European Journal of Applied Physiology*, 112(4), 1429–1436.

Clarke, A.C., Anson, J.M., & Pyne, D.B. (2015a). Physiologically based GPS speed zones for evaluating running demands in women's rugby sevens. *Journal of Sports Sciences*, 33(11), 1101–1108. doi: 10.1080/02640414.2014.988740 [published Online First: 2014/12/17].

Clarke, A.C., Anson, J.M., & Pyne, D.B. (2017). Game movement demands and physical profiles of junior, senior and elite male and female rugby sevens players. *Journal of Sports Sciences*, 35(8), 727–733.

Clarke, A.C., Anson, J.M., & Pyne, D.B. (2015b). Neuromuscular fatigue and muscle damage after a women's rugby sevens tournament. *International Journal of Sports Physiology and Performance*, 10(6), 808–814. doi: 10.1123/ijspp.2014-0590 [published Online First: 2015/04/08].

Couderc, A., Gabbett, T.J., Piscione, J., Robineau, J., Peeters, A., Igarza, G., Thomas, C., Hanon, C., & Lacome, M. (2019). Repeated high-intensity effort activity in international male rugby sevens. *The Journal of Strength & Conditioning Research*. doi: 10.1519/JSC.0000000000002986. [Online ahead of print].

Cummins, C., Orr, R., O'Connor, H., & West, C. (2013). Global positioning systems (GPS) and microtechnology sensors in team sports: A systematic review. *Sports Medicine*, 43(10), 1025–1042.

Cunningham, D.J., Shearer, D.A., Carter, N., Drawer, S., Pollard, B., Bennett, M., Eager, R., Cook, C.J., Farrell, J., Russell, M., & Kilduff, L.P. (2018). Assessing worst case scenarios in movement demands derived from global positioning systems during international rugby union matches: Rolling averages versus fixed length epochs. *PLoS One*, 13(4), e0195197.

Cruz-Ferreira, A.M., Cruz-Ferreira, E.M., Silva, J.D., Ferreira, R.M., Santiago, L.M., & Taborda-Barata, L. (2018). Epidemiology of injuries in Portuguese senior male rugby union sevens: A cohort prospective study. *The Physician and Sportsmedicine*, 46(2), 255–261.

Doeven, S.H., Brink, M.S., Huijgen, B.C., de Jong, J., & Lemmink, K.A. (2019). High match load's relation to decreased well-being during an Elite. *International Journal of Sports Physiology and Performance*, 14(8), 1036–1042.

Emami, F., Kordi Yoosefinejad, A, & Motealleh, A. (2019). Comparison of static and dynamic balance during early follicular and ovulation phases in healthy women, using simple, clinical tests: A cross sectional study. *Gynecol Endocrinol*, 35(3), 257–260.

Fuller, C.W., & Taylor, A. (2020). Ten-season epidemiological study of match injuries in men's international rugby sevens. *Journal of Sports Sciences*, 38(14), 1595–1604. doi: 10.1080/02640414.2020.1752059.

Fuller, C.W., Taylor, A., Kemp, S.P., & Raftery, M. (2017). Rugby World Cup 2015: World rugby injury surveillance study. *British Journal of Sports Medicine*, 51(1), 51–57.

Fuller, C.W., Taylor, A. World Rugby – Surveillance Studies: Sevens World Series (Women). Summary of Results: 2011/12 to 2017/18. In: Rugby W, ed. Dublin. Available at: http://playerwelfare.worldrugby.org, 2018.

Fuller, C.W., Taylor, A.E., & Raftery, M. (2016). Should player fatigue be the focus of injury prevention strategies for international rugby sevens tournaments? *British Journal of Sports Medicine*, 50(11), 682–687.

Goodale, T.L., Gabbett, T.J., Tsai, M.C., Stellingwerff, T., & Sheppard, J. (2017). The effect of contextual factors on physiological and activity profiles in international women's rugby sevens. *International Journal of Sports Physiology and Performance*, 12(3), 370–376.

Hausswirth, C., & Le Meur, Y. (2011). Physiological and nutritional aspects of post-exercise recovery. *Sports Medicine*, 41(10), 861–882.

Hewett, T.E., Myer, G.D., Ford, K.R., Heidt Jr, R.S., Colosimo, A.J., McLean, S.G., van den Bogert, A.J., Paterno, M.V., & Succop, P. (2005). Biomechanical measures of neuromuscular control and valgus loading of the knee predict anterior cruciate ligament injury risk in female athletes: A prospective study. *The American Journal of Sports Medicine*, 33(4), 492–501.

Hewett, T.E., Zazulak, B.T., Myer, G.D., & Ford, K.R. (2005). A review of electromyographic activation levels, timing differences, and increased anterior cruciate ligament injury incidence in female athletes. *British Journal of Sports Medicine*, 39(6), 347–350.

Higham, D.G., Pyne, D.B., Anson, J.M., & Eddy, A. (2012). Movement patterns in rugby sevens: Effects of tournament level, fatigue and substitute players. *Journal of Science and Medicine in Sport*, 15(3), 277–282.

Hunter, S.K. (2016). Sex differences in fatigability of dynamic contractions. *Experimental Physiology*, 101(2), 250–255.

Imwalle, L.E., Myer, G.D., Ford, K.R., & Hewett, T.E. (2009). Relationship between hip and knee kinematics in athletic women during cutting maneuvers: A possible link to noncontact anterior cruciate ligament injury and prevention. *Journal of Strength and Conditioning Research/National Strength & Conditioning Association*, 23(8), 2223.

Jones, T.W., Smith, A., Macnaughton, L.S., & French, D.N. (2016). Strength and conditioning and concurrent training practices in elite rugby union. *The Journal of Strength & Conditioning Research*, 30(12), 3354–3366.

Lacome, M., Piscione, J., Hager, J.P., & Bourdin, M. (2014). A new approach to quantifying physical demand in rugby union. *Journal of Sports Sciences*, 32(3), 290–300.

Malone, S., Earls, M., Shovlin, A., Eddy, A., & Winkelman, N. (2020). Match-play running performance and exercise intensity in elite international women's rugby sevens. *The Journal of Strength & Conditioning Research*, 34(6), 1741–1749. doi: 10.1519/JSC.0000000000002547.

McGowan, C.J., Pyne, D.B., Thompson, K.G., & Rattray, B. (2015). Warm-up strategies for sport and exercise: Mechanisms and applications. *Sports Medicine*, 45(11), 1523–1546.

Nicholas, C.W. (1997). Anthropometric and physiological characteristics of rugby union football players. *Sports Medicine*, 23(6), 375–396.

Peeters, A., Carling, C., Piscione, J., & Lacome, M. (2019). In-match physical performance fluctuations in international rugby sevens competition. *Journal of Sports Science & Medicine*, 18(3), 419.

Portillo, J., González-Ravé, J.M., Juárez, D., García, J.M., Suárez-Arrones, L., & Newton, R.U. (2014). Comparison of running characteristics and heart rate response of international and national female rugby sevens players during competitive matches. *The Journal of Strength & Conditioning Research*, 28(8), 2281–2289.

Reyneke, J., Hansen, K., Cronin, J.B., & Macadam, P. (2018). An investigation into the influence of score differential on the physical demands of international women's rugby sevens match play. *International Journal of Performance Analysis in Sport*, 18(4), 523–531.

Ross, A., Gill, N., & Cronin, J. (2014). Match analysis and player characteristics in rugby sevens. *Sports Medicine*, 44(3), 357–367.

Ruby, B.C., & Robergs, R.A. (1994). Gender differences in substrate utilisation during exercise. *Sports Medicine*, 17(6), 393–410.

Sella, F.S., McMaster, D.T., Beaven, C.M., Gill, N.D., & Hébert-Losier, K. (2019). Match demands, anthropometric characteristics, and physical qualities of female rugby sevens athletes: A systematic review. *The Journal of Strength & Conditioning Research*, 33(12), 3463–3474.

Sewright, K.A., Hubal, M.J., Kearns, A., Holbrook, M.T., & Clarkson, P.M. (2008). Sex differences in response to maximal eccentric exercise. *Medicine & Science in Sports & Exercise*, 40, 242–251.

Shephard, R.J. (2000). Exercise and training in women, Part I: Influence of gender on exercise and training responses. *Canadian Journal of Applied Physiology*, 25(1), 19–34.

Sheppy, E., Hills, S.P., Russell, M., Chambers, R., Cunningham, D.J., Shearer, D., Heffernan, S., Waldron, M., McNarry, M., & Kilduff, L.P. (2020). Assessing the whole-match and worst-case scenario locomotor demands of international women's rugby union match-play. *Journal of Science and Medicine in Sport*, 23(6), 609–614.

Snyder, A.C. (1998). Overtraining and glycogen depletion hypothesis. *Medicine and Science in Sports and Exercise*, 30(7), 1146–1150.

Suarez-Arrones, L., Nuñez, F.J., Portillo, J., & Mendez-Villanueva, A. (2012). Match running performance and exercise intensity in elite female rugby sevens. *The Journal of Strength & Conditioning Research*, 26(7), 1858–1862.

Suarez-Arrones, L., Portillo, J., Pareja-Blanco, F., de Villareal, E.S., Sánchez-Medina, L., & Munguía-Izquierdo, D. (2014). Match-play activity profile in elite women's rugby union players. *The Journal of Strength & Conditioning Research*, 28(2), 452–458.

Taylor, A.E., Fuller, C.W., & Molloy, M.G. (2011). Injury surveillance during the 2010 IRB Women's Rugby World Cup. *British Journal of Sports Medicine*, 45(15), 1243–1245.

Vescovi, J.D., & Goodale, T. (2015). Physical demands of women's rugby sevens matches: Female athletes in motion (FAiM) study. *International Journal of Sports Medicine*, 94(11), 887–892.

5 Collective efficiency and performance in women's rugby sevens

Guillaume Saulière, Quentin DeLarochelambert and Adrien Sedeaud

Rugby is a collective, contact sport – like any other team sport, it involves multiple players with countless interactions among themselves. It is understood that individual experience is an important determinant for a team to perform well (Saulière et al., 2019). However, only a few studies have successfully analyzed players' experience individually in relation to collective performance, as it is challenging to quantify all the events that happen in one game.

The performance of individual players contributes to the team performance; furthermore, it is the construction of the collective that leads the team to win. Indeed, some studies have shown the importance of investigating cohesion and collective efficacy factors as the key performance indicators in team sports (Bourbousson et al., 2010; Fransen et al., 2015; Heuzé et al., 2006; Leo et al., 2013; Marcos et al., 2010; Sedeaud et al., 2017). Such studies also show that previous success is one of the most important indicators of future success (Mukherjee et al., 2019).

Existing literature highlights that a team requires highly skilled players as well as cooperative teammates (Mukherjee et al., 2019). For example, teams that include forwards with previous World Cup experience perform better (Sedeaud et al., 2012). However, most of the previous studies have assessed such experience by simply adding up the number of games played or other athlete characteristics, and not in a collective way (Shearer, 2015).

One study has performed analyses on the collective effectiveness of the French national rugby team, which shows that a team with more experienced forward players leads the overall performance of halfback, lock and center players (Sedeaud et al., 2017). Other studies also analysed the impact of player-turnover rates on the final result in rugby union and football. According to such studies, for the French national rugby team, a turnover rate of more than 40% in two consecutive games is associated with a higher loss percentage for the following game when compared to a turnover rate of lower than 30% (Sedeaud et al., 2017). A similar result was replicated in football by Carling et al. (2015). Additionally, some studies demonstrated that players with more game experience not only have better individual results but also are considered to be more efficient in team performance (Fransen et al., 2015; Heuzé et al., 2006; Leo et al., 2013). A number of studies have investigated the individual performance of players as related to team performance (Fewell et al., 2012; Duch et al., 2010). For example, Duch et al. (2010) quantified the impact of each member's experience on team performance to provide an estimate of individual contributions and the overall team performance. In other existing literature, general network analysis has been performed to study the network characteristics of successful and unsuccessful national teams and to understand the interaction among members of a sports team (Mukherjee, 2013).

In rugby, as in other collective sports, a team's performance cannot be described by the simple sum of its players' skills or their performance. The quality of performance of this collective contact sport depends on coordination based on shared knowledge, action and both positive and negative game experiences through the time spent together as a team. For rugby union, collective experience can be quantified based on the cumulative shared selections (CSS) of players, which allows researchers to assess its impact on team performance; it is understood that the slope of CSS is significantly associated with winning percentage (Saulière et al., 2019). CSS also indicates the progression of a team's experience and is linked to performance through game (Saulière et al., 2019). As demonstrated in basketball, football, baseball and cricket, it is likely that the higher the team CSS, the better its future performance (Mukherjee et al., 2019).

International rugby sevens has a unique competition style where all the players must participate at some point during the two days of competition. Such a formation leads to a shorter length of game period, where players must be physically, technically and collectively ready to perform as a team. In contrast to rugby union, this condition leaves rugby sevens players with much less time to build collective experience (Saulière et al., 2019; Sedeaud et al., 2017; Sedeaud et al., 2012). As understood, the game dynamic is different by game and by team (Carreras et al., 2013; Higham et al., 2012). In addition, rugby sevens has a short effective time and relatively small numbers of events happening in one game. Based on these two factors, coaches are required to develop an effective tactic that maximises the coordination among players and that leads to a better collective performance (Doeven et al., 2019). Like rugby union, it is assumed that shared time as a team is an important factor to maximise the players' coordination in rugby sevens. In fact, the increase in collective experience is presumably associated with international ranking and overall winning rate. However, most of the studies that look into collective effectiveness and performance are performed on men's rugby sevens, and rarely on women's. More studies on women's rugby sevens are needed in order to correctly identify and describe the number and sequence of events that happen in one game.

Modelling of sports events as a continuation of transitions from one state to another is an increasingly used methodology. A recent review by Claudino et al. revealed that the Markov process is indeed the third most commonly used tool, just after artificial neural networks and the decision tree classifier, in studies that use artificial intelligence for performance prediction (Claudino et al., 2019; Pfeiffer et al., 2010). Most of such studies were in the "technical and tactical analysis" field of team sports that is aimed at predicting a winning team (Claudino et al., 2019; Pfeiffer et al., 2010; Halouani et al., 2014; Valero, 2016; Kvam & Sokol 2006; Kolbush & Sokol, 2017; Tümer & Koçer, 2017; Demers, 2015; Leicht et al., 2017). Several studies have also focused on assessing the reliability of technical and tactical analysis in combat sports, highlighting the contribution that Markov models can make (Ashker, 2011; López-González & Miarka, 2013; Thomson et al., 2013; Miarka et al., 2015).

The purpose of this chapter is to understand the impact of collective experience on the success of a team and to analyse its chances of winning or losing according to the events occurring during matches.

Methods

Data collection

Data were collected from the World Rugby website: www.worldrugby.org. Scoresheets of all international women's sevens rugby games were obtained for every year from the 2012 IRB Women's Sevens World Series in Dubai to the 2019 HSBC World Rugby Women's Sevens Series in Biarritz. The date of the game, the name of tournament, points scored and conceded, and names and positions of players put as starting members were recorded for each international game. Score timelines describing who scored a try and when were collected when available.

Team experience indicator: cumulative shared selections

In this study, CSS was created based on the list of the starting members selected by the head coach. For each game, the number of games that each player shared with other players during the previous games was computed and added up as follows.

A network for each national team was defined with n vertices corresponding to every player selected over m matches through a certain period of time. A different vertex could or could not be linked by edge E, depending on whether players shared at least one game or not. All the edges were weighted according to the number of matches shared by players: if two players i and j (i and $j \in \{1,...,n\}$) played in a given match k ($k \in \{1,...,m\}$), then $E^k_{i,j} = 1$. If they did not play together or only one played, then $E^k_{i,j} = 0$.

Therefore, the formula to quantify the number of the CSS of one team at a given game g ($g \in \{1,...,m\}$) is

$$CSS_g = \frac{1}{2} \times \sum_{k=1}^{g-1}\left(\sum_{i=1}^{n}\left(\sum_{j=1,j\neq i}^{n}\left(E^k_{i,j}\right)\right)\right).$$

Multiplication by ½ is required in order not to consider the same interaction twice [i.e., couples $(i = 1, j = 2)$ and $(i = 2, j = 1)$]. By applying this formula, CSS was computed for all 32 nations over the entire study period.

Performance indicators

Team performance was quantified by (1) total points scored and conceded at the end of each match and (2) the evolution of the score throughout the match. When the progression of the score was available, all of the points scored and conceded by the team were summed up. For each game, we randomly designed one team playing as team a and the other as team b. Thirteen different states were defined to describe the progression of a game, and for the purpose of analysis, the baseline state was set as *tie*. Out of the 13 states, five states were defined accordingly: when team a (a) took the lead (*aTL*, can happen during the game whenever the score is tied and one team takes the lead); increased its lead (*aIL*); turned the game around (*aTA*); conceded a try yet kept leading (*aCyL*); and equalised (*aE*). Another five states were defined in contrast: when team b (b) took the lead (*bTL*); increased its lead (*bIL*); turned the game around (*bTA*); conceded a try yet kept leading (*bCyl*); and equalised (*bE*). Lastly, the remaining two states were defined as team a wins (*W*) and team b loses (*L*).

Statistical analysis

For each game, CSS and score differences were computed between teams. First, a variable *CSS difference* was created and defined as "more" when the CSS difference was positive and "less" when the difference was negative. Then, the score difference was analyzed according to this binary variable. Results are presented in Figure 5.1 as a box plot, with means represented by a solid horizontal line.

Efficiency and performance in rugby sevens 63

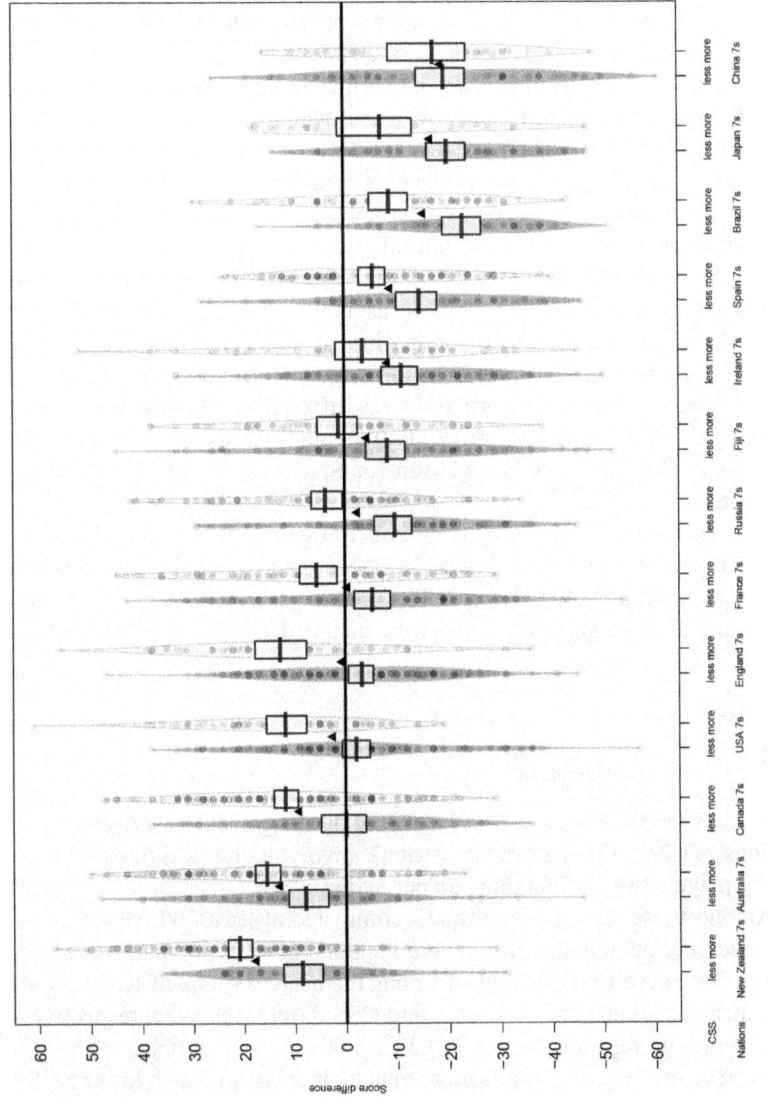

Figure 5.1 Score differences according to number of CSS

For the performance indicator, a multistates model was used to describe the progression of games characterised by the score (state) as a function of time. $R(t)$ is the state of the game at time t, and the likelihood for this model is calculated from the transition probability matrix, $P(n,t+n)$. In addition, $P_{r,s}(n,t+n)$ is the probability of being in the state s at a time $t+n$, with the baseline assumption of a state at the time n is r. The transition matrix used by the model, $P(n,t+n)$, contains transition probabilities, which are computed empirically with the available data, of moving from one state to another – from one instant t to $t+n$. By defining transitions for each game, the progression of scores makes it possible to illustrate and model the interaction between two variables of interest (state and time).

Transition matrices are represented as chord diagrams in Figures 5.2.1 and 5.2.2, which illustrate transition probabilities between the different states. Figures 5.2.3 and 5.2.4 represent the change of proportion in all matches in different states over time. Data are reported as mean ± standard deviation. Linear regression was performed to test the potential association between score and CSS differences. Results are considered significant at $p < 0.05$. All statistical analyses were performed with R (version 3.6.1; The R Foundation for Statistical Computing, Vienna, Austria).

It is clear that CSS varies by the number of games each nation played – if a nation played only a few games, its CSS would be smaller than that of a nation that completed ten games. To minimise such a bias, nations with a minimum of 100 completed games were included in this part of the analysis.

Results

CSS and score differences

The study period of 2012–2019 covered 1,459 games played among 32 nations (91.2 ± 95.0 games per nation), involving 1,158 different female rugby players (35.1 ± 20.0 players per nation).

Among those 32 nations, only 13 completed at least 100 games during the study period and, therefore, were included in the CSS analysis. During this period, these 13 teams played among themselves a total of 1,160 games. The mean absolute values of score and CSS differences were, respectively, 16.7 ± 11.7 points and 254.9 ± 249.3 CSS. Teams with a higher CSS score an average of 19.1 ± 7.1 points more than their opponents with lower a CSS. In addition, 64.1% of winning teams had a higher CSS number than their opponent, whereas only 35.9% of winning teams had a lower CSS number than their opponent. In linear regression, CSS difference is found to be significantly associated with score difference $\left(p\text{ value} < 0.001, R^2 = 0.20\right)$.

Efficiency and performance in rugby sevens 65

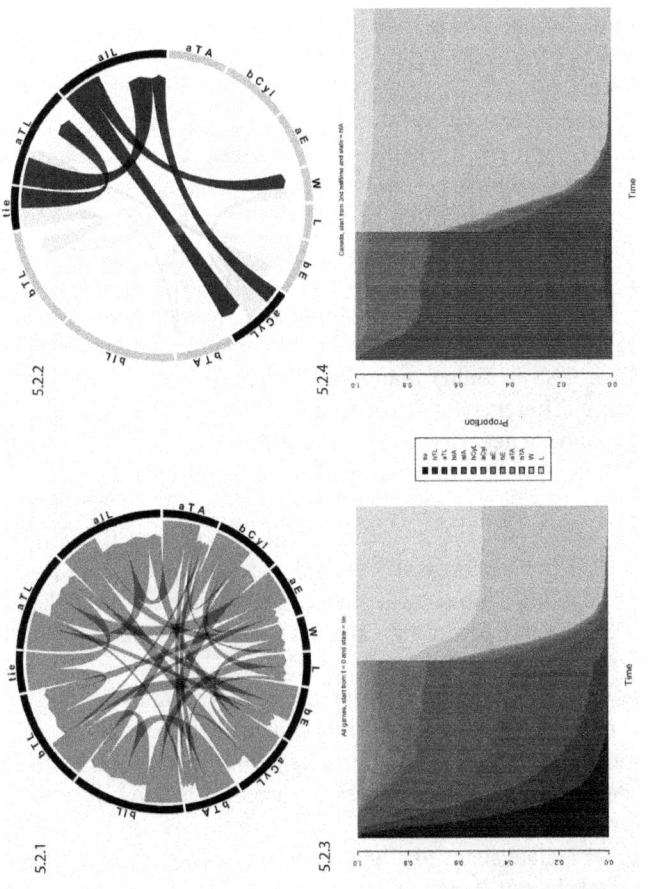

Figure 5.2 Results and illustrations of the multistates model

5.2.1 displays the probability (proportionally to the thickness of the arrow) of entering the next state (end of the arrow) from the starting state (start of the arrow). 5.2.2 illustrates the course of a match as a sequence of transitions from one state to another. 5.2.3 illustrates the change of proportion in all the matches (total of 1,459 games) in different states over time. 5.2.4 illustrates the transitioning of states of the Canadian team.

Figure 5.1 illustrates the score differences of the 13 nations of interest. This figure shows that if teams have a higher CSS than their opponent, they have an average higher score difference, while if they have a lower CSS than their opponent, they have a lower score difference. The 13 nations are sorted from left to right in accordance with their mean score difference over the study period.

As shown, New Zealand is on the far left with the highest score difference (17.7 ± 15.8 points), and China is on the far right with the lowest score difference (−18.9 ± 19.05 points). From the example of New Zealand and Australia, which are top-performing nations with higher mean score differences, it is clear that such high-level nations win more often and with a wider range of score difference when they have more collective experience than their opponents. Similarly, Japan, China, Brazil and Spain, rather low-performing teams, may lose often but with a smaller range of score difference when they have more collective experience than their opponents. Moreover, France and Russia show, on average, negative score differences when they have a lower CSS and inversely a positive average score difference when they have a higher CSS than their opponents. France and Russia show that when their CSS is higher than that of their opponent, they have a positive mean score difference, and when their CSS is lower than that of their opponent, they have a negative mean score difference.

Multistates analysis

Unlike CSS analysis, team performance analysis was computed based on all 1,459 games by applying a multistates model. Every game was modelled through the perspective of the home team and the away team to have a winner and a loser for each game.

Figure 5.2.1 shows the probability of a game (in proportion to the thickness of the arrow) entering the next state (end of the arrow) from the previous state (beginning of the arrow). The intermediate states that exist the most often are when one team (a or b team), currently leading, has just scored and therefore increased its lead (characterised by states aIL and bIL). There were two intermediate states that had the highest probability of transitioning into the final state of W, which are increased its lead (aIL, 0.4) and conceded a try yet kept leading ($aCyl$, 0.3).

Figure 5.2.2 illustrates the course of a match as a sequence of transitions from one state to another. It starts with the score baseline *tie*, and then team a scores the first try and takes the lead (aTL). Then team a scores again and increases its advantage (aIL). Its opponent, team b, scores its first try, yet team a keeps the advantage ($aCyl$). Finally, the match ends, and team a wins the game (W).

Figure 5.2.3 illustrates the change of proportion in all the matches (total of 1,459 games) in different states over time. At baseline, all the games were in the state *tie*. Then, they gradually transitioned into different states over time and reached the final states of W or L at the end. According to the figure, we can see that 34% of the games had already reached the final state at 14 min into the game. After 14 minutes, all the games transitioned into either one of the two final states and none of the intermediate states – the longest recorded match lasted 26 minutes. By sequencing a match according to defined states, it was possible to predict results with better accuracy, and Figure 5.2.4 is one such example. Figure 5.2.4 illustrates the transitioning of states of the Canadian team. The figure represents all 84 games played by the Canadian team, where Canada is in the state of scored and increasing its lead at the beginning of the second half (time = 7 min). Under this circumstance, 94.05% of the games ended with the Canadian team winning. We can see that a large proportion (70.24% at 14 min) of games remained in or went back to this current state up to reaching the final state *win*. Through time we can see the proportion of games in the state conceded a try yet kept leading increasing to the maximum of 26.19% after 6 minutes and 7 seconds of play in the second half.

Discussion

This chapter quantifies and analyses a collective performance indicator that seems important for understanding the success of a team. To deepen our knowledge, the influence of current events on the final result of a match was also analysed.

Rugby sevens is a sport with a short playing time (14 minutes) that leaves little time for players to adapt to a constantly changing environment – players must be collectively ready to perform as soon as the whistle blows. Many studies suggest that collective experience is one of the most crucial factors for better team performance (Bourbousson et al., 2010; Fransen et al., 2015; Heuzé et al., 2006; Leo et al., 2013; Marcos et al., 2010; Sedeaud et al., 2017; Mukherjee et al., 2019; Sedeaud et al., 2012; Shearer, 2015). Team cohesion and collective efficiency are widely used to quantify collective experience (Bourbousson et al., 2010; Fransen et al., 2015; Heuzé et al., 2006). Teams can build up collective experience through the time players share with one another in practice and games (Shearer, 2015).

Cumulative experience

The results show that regardless of the overall performance quality, the time shared during competition (CSS) by all players is associated with team performance – the higher the CSS, the better the team performance. The results in women's rugby sevens are consistent with those in rugby union, which confirms that CSS remains relevant despite the fact that sevens has a shorter game length (Saulière et al., 2019). Through this study, CSS is determined to be a good measurement to quantify the overall progress of team performance and, therefore, could become a potential variable to look at during training. Nonetheless, a continuous improvement in CSS over a long period of time is in question as it implies a general ageing of the group (Saulière et al., 2019). Repeated sprinting, changes of direction in running, accelerations and decelerations are required key skills of rugby sevens players, which require young athletes. To maximise tactical group cohesion and optimal operation, coaches and directors normally bring together experienced athletes and young athletes who are at the peak of their physical performance (Saulière et al., 2019).

Importance of capitalised experience

The length of a game in rugby sevens is only 14 minutes, and each nation participates in five to eight tournaments per year depending on the number of tournaments organised in one season. Under such circumstances, teams must capitalise on every single opportunity to develop collective experience. Mean effective playing time per player in five games was 10.8 ± 5.9 minutes per game for elite women's rugby sevens (Doeven et al., 2019). Other studies on elite men's rugby sevens games report a mean playing time of 16.3 ± 1.0 minutes for players playing the whole game and 7.9 ± 3.5 minutes for interchanged players (Couderc et al., 2017). In elite women's rugby sevens, players run $1,556 \pm 189$ m on average at an average speed of 6.8 ± 0.6 m s^{-1} and complete 5.3 ± 1.6 sprints on average (Suarez-Arrones et al., 2016; Ross et al., 2015; Suarez-Arrones et al., 2014). Regarding men's rugby sevens performance, it has been reported that players take, on average, 3.2 ± 2.5 ball carries, 2.4 ± 2.3 tackles and 2.3 ± 3.9 total rucks (Ross et al., 2015). Finally, over 90% of ball-in-play sequences during men's rugby sevens matches last less than 60 seconds, with an average sequence length of 28 seconds in Pool play and 33 seconds in Cup play (Schuster et al., 2018). Players must have complete knowledge of each other in order to achieve better coordination, allowing them to rightly form and clear rucks, complete key passes at high speed or perform offloads. As previously mentioned, players' interactions during games do not occur a lot. Consequently, coaches need to consider not only their athletes' individual development but also their collective interplay and cohesion.

Influence of prior events on team performance

Reflecting the shorter game length of rugby sevens and its consequences, this study investigated the influence of events within the game on the final result of a match based on a Markov process. A multistate model was chosen because it makes it possible to compute the transition probabilities of all states that influence the game as well as the final result. Existing studies focused on estimating rugby performance by using game results as a performance indicator, but not the evolution of the score through its varying states. We defined 13 different states, of which ten intermediate states include information from the previous state. For example, the state increased its lead (aIL) for team a implies that team a was leading – in a positive dynamic. These states are reflected in Figure 5.2.1, which shows the probability of entering the next state from a starting state. It shows that there is no possible transition from the state aIL to the final state team a loses (L). Yet it is possible to reach the state team a wins (W) from state $aCyL$. Another primary result is that there is a very high probability of reaching state aIL from state aTL, meaning that in rugby sevens, the team scoring the first try has a great chance to keep its advantage until the end of the game. This finding is reflected in Figure 5.2.4, illustrating that 94.05% of the time the Canadian team was in the winning state (W) when they were in state aIL at halftime. Our results also show a high probability of transition from state aIL to $aCyL$ and vice versa, yet a null probability of losing the game from the state aIL. Moreover, in Figure 5.2.4, it is apparent that even if 26% of the game could be in the state $aCyL$ at 13.7 minutes, 94% of the game would still result in the winning state. These two observations combined may put into numbers the moment at which a team leading by a large score seals the game and opts to ease off the pace slightly.

Perspectives

Information provided by the number of CSS is macroscopic: it shows the existing relationships between all the players in a team. However, further research focused on producing a microscopic analysis of the relationships between the players is needed. Social network analysis (SNA) may be a useful tool to provide a deeper investigation as it can be used to study the behaviours of players and their interactions with their teammates as well as with opponents during a match (Grund, 2012; Araújo & Davids, 2016; Cintia et al., 2016; Guillaume & Latapy, 2004; Pina et al., 2017). In this context, network nodes (players) as well as their interactions (passes, contacts, movement coordinates) provide a framework for performance modelling by identifying the impact of key pass-chains, main actors and major events (try, replacement, exclusion, etc.) on the specific design of each of these networks. Based on this framework, collective experience among identified players could be associated with specific performance indicators. Moreover, this framework makes it possible to test the strengths and weaknesses of a particular association of players in a predefined situation and facing certain opponents.

Modelling of sports events as a succession of transitions from one state to another is a methodology increasingly being used, which relies on stochastic models (Pfeiffer et al., 2010). Indeed, Kvam and Sokol (2006) used such a process to predict the winner of National Collegiate Athletic Association (NCAA) basketball games. In this study, each team was defined as one state, and transition probabilities were adjusted based on the teams' past performances; all the teams were ranked in accordance with the stationary distribution of the model. In addition, Shirley (2007) applied the Markov model with states that corresponded to how a team obtained ball possession and the number of points scored during the previous transition. The study completed by Thomson et al. (2013) confirmed that Markov modelling can also be applied to boxing and identified 25 performance indicators to predict game results. Miarka et al. (2015) applied a multistate model in judo. Their work estimated the probabilities of transition among states during combat, where each state was defined by a phase of combat (e.g., attack, defense, etc.), which influences winning through indicators such as combat time, points scored, penalties and attack orientations.

Markov processes seem to be the most appropriate tool for analysing such sequences in order to promote better understanding of how these events follow one another and how they impact the outcome of the matches. It has been suggested that covariate(s) be added to the multistates model for future studies. Addition of covariates (such as collective experience indicators, threshold in score differences, age of players and market value of teams) could be a valuable source of information, significantly improving the predictive power of the model.

Conclusion

This chapter presents two different methods relevant to collective performance, which has not been done in previous studies on women's rugby. By using such methods, the association between CSS and overall team performance was identified. Then, the multistate Markov model was applied to understand the transitioning of states that lead to the final result of either winning or losing. This analysis provided information on the probability of future events, such as which team would be scoring the next try. Both analyses produced additional understanding of better practice of high-level rugby and suggested that CSS and Markov modelling could be advantageous in the decision-making process in competitive analysis.

Acknowledgements

We deeply thank Moï Yamazaki for reviewing the manuscript and providing language help.

References

Araújo, D., & Davids, K. (2016). Team synergies in sport: Theory and measures. *Frontiers in Psychology*, 7, 1449.

Ashker, S.E. (2011). Technical and tactical aspects that differentiate winning and losing performances in boxing. *International Journal of Performance Analysis in Sport*, 11(2), 356–364.

Bourbousson, J., Poizat, G., Saury, J., & Seve, C. (2010). Team coordination in basketball: Description of the cognitive connections among teammates. *Journal of Applied Sport Psychology*, 22(2), 150–166.

Carling, C., Le Gall, F., McCall, A., Nédélec, M., & Dupont, G. (2015). Squad management, injury and match performance in a professional soccer team over a championship-winning season. *European Journal of Sport Science*, 15(7), 573–582.

Carreras, D., Kraak, W., Planas, A., Martín, I., & Vaz, L. (2013). Analysis of international rugby sevens matches during tournaments. *International Journal of Performance Analysis in Sport*, 13(3), 833–847.

Cintia, P., Coscia, M., & Pappalardo, L. (2016, August). The Haka network: Evaluating rugby team performance with dynamic graph analysis. In *2016 IEEE/ACM International Conference on Advances in Social Networks Analysis and Mining (ASONAM)*. San Francisco: IEEE, pp. 1095–1102.

Claudino, J.G., de Oliveira Capanema, D., de Souza, T.V., Serrão, J.C., Pereira, A.C.M., & Nassis, G.P. (2019). Current approaches to the use of artificial intelligence for injury risk assessment and performance prediction in team sports: A systematic review. *Sports Medicine-Open*, 5(1), 28.

Couderc, A., Thomas, C., Lacome, M., Piscione, J., Robineau, J., Delfour-Peyrethon, R., Borne, R., & Hanon, C. (2017). Movement patterns and metabolic responses during an international rugby sevens tournament. *International Journal of Sports Physiology and Performance*, 12(7), 901–907.

Demers, S. (2015). Riding a probabilistic support vector machine to the Stanley Cup. *Journal of Quantitative Analysis in Sports*, 11(4), 205–218.

Doeven, S.H., Brink, M.S., Huijgen, B.C., de Jong, J., & Lemmink, K.A. (2019). High match load's relation to decreased well-being during an elite women's rugby sevens tournament. *International Journal of Sports Physiology and Performance*, 14(8), 1036–1042.

Duch, J., Waitzman, J.S., & Amaral, L.A.N. (2010). Quantifying the performance of individual players in a team activity. *PLoS One*, 5(6), e10937.

Fewell, J.H., Armbruster, D., Ingraham, J., Petersen, A., & Waters, J.S. (2012). Basketball teams as strategic networks. *PLoS One*, 7(11), e47445.

Fransen, K., Decroos, S., Vanbeselaere, N., Vande Broek, G., De Cuyper, B., Vanroy, J., & Boen, F. (2015). Is team confidence the key to success? The reciprocal relation between collective efficacy, team outcome confidence, and perceptions of team performance during soccer games. *Journal of Sports Sciences*, 33(3), 219–231.

Grund, T.U. (2012). Network structure and team performance: The case of English Premier League soccer teams. *Social Networks*, 34(4), 682–690.

Guillaume, J.L., & Latapy, M. (2004). Bipartite structure of all complex networks. *Information Processing Letters*, 90(5), 215–221.

Halouani, J., Chtourou, H., Gabbett, T., Chaouachi, A., & Chamari, K. (2014). Small-sided games in team sports training: A brief review. *The Journal of Strength & Conditioning Research*, 28(12), 3594–3618.

Heuzé, J.P., Raimbault, N., & Fontayne, P. (2006). Relationships between cohesion, collective efficacy and performance in professional basketball teams: An examination of mediating effects. *Journal of Sports Sciences*, 24(1), 59–68.

Higham, D.G., Pyne, D.B., Anson, J.M., & Eddy, A. (2012). Movement patterns in rugby sevens: Effects of tournament level, fatigue and substitute players. *Journal of Science and Medicine in Sport*, 15(3), 277–282.

Kolbush, J., & Sokol, J. (2017). A logistic regression/Markov chain model for American college football. *International Journal of Computer Science in Sport*, 16(3), 185–196.

Kvam, P., & Sokol, J.S. (2006). A logistic regression/Markov chain model for NCAA basketball. *Naval Research Logistics*, 53(8), 788–803.

Leicht, A.S., Gómez, M.A., & Woods, C.T. (2017). Explaining match outcome during the men's basketball tournament at the Olympic Games. *Journal of Sports Science & Medicine*, 16(4), 468.

Leo, F.M., Sánchez-Miguel, P.A., Sánchez-Oliva, D., Amado, D., & García-Calvo, T. (2013). Analysis of cohesion and collective efficacy profiles for the performance of soccer players. *Journal of Human Kinetics*, 39(1), 221–229.

López-González, D.E., & Miarka, B. (2013). Reliability of a new time-motion analysis model based on technical-tactical interactions for wrestling competition. *International Journal of Wrestling Science*, 3(1), 21–34.

Marcos, F.M.L., Miguel, P.A.S., Oliva, D.S., & Calvo, T.G. (2010). Interactive effects of team cohesion on perceived efficacy in semi-professional sport. *Journal of Sports Science & Medicine*, 9(2), 320.

Miarka, B., Branco, B.H., Vecchio, F.B., Camey, S., & Franchini, E. (2015). Development and validation of a time-motion judo combat model based on the Markovian processes. *International Journal of Performance Analysis in Sport*, 15(1), 315–331.

Mukherjee, S. (2013). Complex network analysis in cricket: Community structure, player's role and performance index. *Advances in Complex Systems*, 16(8), 1350031-1:1350031-20.

Mukherjee, S., Huang, Y., Neidhardt, J., Uzzi, B., & Contractor, N. (2019). Prior shared success predicts victory in team competitions. *Nature Human Behaviour*, 3(1), 74–81.

Pfeiffer, M., Zhang, H., & Hohmann, A. (2010). A Markov chain model of elite table tennis competition. *International Journal of Sports Science & Coaching*, 5(2), 205–222.

Pina, T.J., Paulo, A., & Araújo, D. (2017). Network characteristics of successful performance in association football. A study on the UEFA Champions League. *Frontiers in Psychology*, 8, 1173.

Ross, A., Gill, N.D., & Cronin, J.B. (2015). A comparison of the match demands of international and provincial rugby sevens. *International Journal of Sports Physiology and Performance*, 10(6), 786–790.

Saulière, G., Jérôme, D., Moussa, I., Schipman, J., Toussaint, J.F., & Sedeaud, A. (2019). Quantifying collective performance in rugby union. *Frontiers in Sports and Active Living*, 1, 44.

Schuster, J., Howells, D., Robineau, J., Couderc, A., Natera, A., Lumley, N., . . . Winkelman, N. (2018). Physical-preparation recommendations for elite rugby sevens performance. *International Journal of Sports Physiology and Performance*, 13(3), 255–267.

Sedeaud, A., Marc, A., Schipman, J., Tafflet, M., Hager, J.P., & Toussaint, J.F. (2012). How they won Rugby World Cup through height, mass and collective experience. *British Journal of Sports Medicine*, 46(8), 580–584.

Sedeaud, A., Saulière, G., Marquet, L.A., Del Vecchio, S., Bar-Hen, A., & Toussaint, J.F. (2017). Collective effectiveness in the XV de France: Selections and time matter. *European Journal of Sport Science*, 17(6), 656–664.

Shearer, D.A. (2015). Collective efficacy at the Rugby World Cup 2015 – the role of imagery and observation. *European Journal of Sport Science*, 15(6), 530–535.

Shirley, K. (2007, September). A Markov model for basketball. In *New England Symposium for Statistics in Sports*, pp. 82–82, Cambridge, Massachusetts.

Suarez-Arrones, L., Arenas, C., López, G., Requena, B., Terrill, O., & Mendez-Villanueva, A. (2014). Positional differences in match running performance and physical collisions in men rugby sevens. *International Journal of Sports Physiology and Performance*, 9(2), 316–323.

Suarez-Arrones, L., Núñez, J., de Villareal, E.S., Gálvez, J., Suarez-Sanchez, G., & Munguía-Izquierdo, D. (2016). Repeated-high-intensity-running activity and internal training load of elite rugby sevens players during international matches: A comparison between halves. *International Journal of Sports Physiology and Performance*, 11(4), 495–499.

Thomson, E., Lamb, K., & Nicholas, C. (2013). The development of a reliable amateur boxing performance analysis template. *Journal of Sports Sciences*, 31(5), 516–528.

Tümer, A.E., & Koçer, S. (2017). Prediction of team league's rankings in volleyball by artificial neural network method. *International Journal of Performance Analysis in Sport*, 17(3), 202–211.

Valero, C.S. (2016). Predicting win-loss outcomes in MLB regular season games – a comparative study using data mining methods. *International Journal of Computer Science in Sport*, 15(2), 91–112.

6 Evolution of social cohesion within a national rugby union team

Helene Joncheray, Renaud Laporte and Pauline Maillot

Connections between cohesion and sport performance have been highlighted by numerous scholars (Carron et al., 2002; Heuzé et al., 2007; Jacob & Carron, 1998; Terborg et al., 1976), but few have explored the evolution over time of cohesion among elite teams (Carless, 2000; Carron & Brawley, 2000; Stevenson & Durand-Bush, 1999). However, cohesion is a dynamic process changing over time (Bandura, 1977; Carron & Eys, 2012; Leo et al., 2015). Moreover, cohesion is not self-evident: cooperation, even within a collective sport team – in which several players can claim to play a certain position, for instance – can entail rivalries. This is even truer for national teams, which are made up of players from different clubs who can thus be opponents during the rest of the year. Group dynamics are also influenced by the coaches, who select (i.e., the number of selections) and start certain players on the team or leave them on the bench (Spink, 1992), among others. These dynamics affect the team's cohesion.

Two main schools of thought oppose each other on the analysis of cohesion: those who advocate a unidimensional conception of cohesion (Back, 1951; Festinger et al., 1950; Lott & Lott, 1965; Schachter, 1951; Schachter et al., 1951) and those who advance a multidimensional model (Bollen & Hoyle, 1990; Carron et al., 1985; Cota et al., 1995; Hogg & Hardie, 1991). However, in the majority of studies, scholars agree to put forward two dimensions of cohesion, namely, task cohesion and social cohesion (Back, 1951; Leo Marcos et al., 2012; Mikalachki, 1969; Van Bergen & Koelebakker, 1959). Task cohesion exists when the group coheres around the task it was organised to perform, while social cohesion exists when the group coheres around social (nontask) functions. Social cohesion "reflects the degree to which team members empathize with each other and enjoy the companionship of the group" (Leo Marcos et al., 2012, p. 130). The distinction between these two forms of cohesion – task cohesion, a functional or practical form of cohesion (Widmeyer et al., 1985), and social cohesion, an interpersonal or socio-affective cohesion (Widmeyer et al., 1985) – proves to be relevant in predicting a group's performance (Buton et al., 2006). Task cohesion is more strongly related to the group's performance during an additional task (Steiner, 1972) than interpersonal cohesion (Zaccaro & Lowe, 1988). But when the task requires interaction between group members – which is the case in our research – the two forms of cohesion are positively related to the group's performance (Carron & Chelladurai, 1981; Zaccaro & McCoy, 1988), especially in women's teams (Carron et al., 2002).

Although cohesion is recognised as multidimensional (Carron et al., 1998; Buton et al., 2006), the choice made in this chapter was to examine only one of the factors put forward in Carron's conceptual model (Carron et al., 1985). We precisely chose to study individual social attractions for the group, which reflect the individual members' feelings related to their social interactions within the group (Carron et al., 1985; Heuzé et al., 2006). These attractions represent a part of perceptions, those tied with the group's social aspects – and not directly with the collective performance – and one of the four factors that affect the development of cohesion in Carron's conceptual model (Carron et al., 1985). Our choice to study one part of cohesion does not oppose the multidimensional model; the issue here was to study the change over time in group and subgroup social cohesion within an elite sports team. Despite the exhaustive research on group-related cohesion (Randsley de Moura et al., 2008), only a few studies analyse the evolution of their cohesion over time (Heuzé et al., 2007; Leo Marcos et al., 2012).

We studied social cohesion within an elite, interactive (Carron et al., 2002) sports team – rugby union – during the Women's Six Nations Championship. Rugby union is an interactive sport with teams comprising 22 players (15 on the field). Eight of them are called the forwards and the other seven are called the backs.

The purpose of this research was to focus on the quantitative changes in the level of perceived social cohesion over time in a group of elite female rugby players (Joncheray et al., 2016). The research was based on the players' relations with the other members of the team. Cohesiveness was studied in relation to three variables: the player's position (back or forward), age and the number of times played for the national team. Starting from this objective, we put forward two hypotheses. The first one focuses on the group taken as a whole and the second one on subgroups constituted according to the three previously mentioned independent variables. The first hypothesis claims that the group's social cohesion evolves positively between the beginning and the end of the six-week competition. The second hypothesis claims that the constitution of subgroups – intragroup (the subgroup's cohesion) and intergroup cohesion (subgroups' appreciation vis-à-vis the other ones) – is mostly the consequence of one variable: the number of selections.

Method

The French national rugby union team studied comprised 30 players over two questionnaire administrations, at T1 and T2. Social cohesion was studied during an international competition lasting six weeks, two days before the first game (T1) and two days before the last one (T2). The questionnaire was administered to the 22 players who had been picked for the match. Because of the coaches' changes to the team during the tournament, the group of 22 players was not the same at T1 and T2. Indeed, 14 players took part in the whole competition and completed the questionnaire twice, at T1 and T2. Eight players only took part in the first two games and eight other players in the last three. The 16 players who participated in a part of the competition completed the questionnaire only once, eight of them before the first match (T1) and the other eight before the last one (T2).

Participants

For each of the two questionnaire administrations, 12 forwards and ten backs completed it. The players' average age was 24.6 years at T1 (SD = 3.3 years) and 23.3 years at T2 (SD = 3.6 years). Ten of the players were under 25 years old at T1 and 14 at T2. Age is positively correlated with the number of selections, $r = 0.80$, $p < .05$. The first time the questionnaire was administered, 14 players had 12 selections or more, which was the case for ten players the second time. These choices – 25 years old or more vs. under 25 years old and 12 selections or more vs. fewer than 12 selections – were made to split the team into two balanced groups for the two groups of 22 players at T1 and T2 as well as for the 14-player group.

Table 6.1 Position played, age and number of selections of the players

	Position played		Age (years)		Number of selections	
	Forward	Back	Under 25	25 and older	Under 12 selections	12 and more
Entire group T1 ($n = 22$)	12	10	10	12	8	14
Entire group T2 ($n = 22$)	12	10	14	8	12	10
Subgroup ($n = 14$)	6	8	6	8	4	10

Measures

Players were asked to fill out a sociometric questionnaire (Deep et al., 1967; Moreno, 1934) pertaining to their perceptions of the social preferences among themselves. Players were told that the objective was not a competitive one but a social one. Cohesiveness was assessed by six questions. The first two had an elective nature (choice, rejection), the next two a perceptive one (expected choices and rejections) and the last two an elective nature (choice and rejection of a leader). The players had to write down which members of the team the players would like or not like to spend time doing a social activity (hiking) with: (1) "Among the players chosen to play for France, which are the ones with whom you would like to form a group to go hiking with?" (2) "Among the team players, which are the ones with whom you would prefer not to form a group to go hiking with?" The designations were ranked according to the order of preference (Moreno, 1934).

Procedure

The two questionnaire administrations were included in the group's activities following a two-day observation period. Every player on the team attended the meeting and participated in the study. The experimenter administered questionnaires after having explained the study. Intense motivation was generated by a real action plan, that is, improving the relations within the group in order to improve performance. The fact that the lead author is a former first-division rugby union player helped build a climate of trust.

The questionnaire data were transferred to Socio1, a sociometric software programme. The cohesion or group interrelation index can vary between −4 and +4. It corresponds to the sum of choices and choice expectations, minus the sum of rejections and expected rejections (what is called the sum of the group's valencies), divided by the number of dyads (or $n(n-1)/2$, n being the number of individuals observed). When we analyse the subgroups, two sorts of indexes emerge: the intragroup indexes and the intergroup indexes. The intragroup index corresponds to the subgroup's cohesion and the intergroup index to the subgroups' appreciation vis-à-vis the other ones.

Data analysis

The players' social cohesion was assessed in relation to their ages, position played and number of national team selections. Each time, we analysed data for the 22-player groups (T1 and T2) and the subgroup of players who participated in the whole competition. For each variable – position played, age and number of selections – t tests were carried out on each of the indexes measured.

Results

First, we present the results for cohesion inside the groups (Table 6.2): intragroup index evolution in the entire group ($n = 22$) and in the 14-player subgroup. We then present results for cohesion between the groups: intergroup index evolution (Table 6.3).

Table 6.2 The intragroup indexes with regard to position played, age and number of selections

	T1	T2	t	p
	General cohesion			
22-player group	0.84	1.02	−1.14	>.26
14-player group	1.38	1.69	−4.43	**<.00****
	Position played			
22-player group				
Backs group	1.31	1.57	−1.01	>.32
Forwards group	0.83	0.84	−0.06	>.95
14-player group				
Backs group	1.46	1.64	−1.73	>.12
Forwards group	1.80	2.33	−4.00	**<.02***
	Age (years)			
22-player group				
Players 25 and older	1.21	2.00	−3.36	**<.01***
Players under 25	0.95	0.68	1.65	>.11
14-player group				
Players 25 and older	1.53	2.00	−3.55	**<.01***
Players under 25	1.26	1.00	1.35	>.23
	Number of selections			
22-player group				
12 selections and more	1.43	2.40	−4.32	**<.00****
Fewer than 12 selections	1.42	0.77	3.08	**<.02***
14-player group				
12 selections and more	2.08	2.40	−3.28	**<.01***
Fewer than 12 selections	0.50	1.16	−2.82	>.06

* $p < .05$
** $p < .01$

Table 6.3 The intergroup indexes with regard to position played, age and number of selections

	T1	T2	t	p
	Position played			
22-player group	0.68	0.91	−1.13	>.26
14-player group	1.20	1.52	−1.53	>.13
	Age			
22-player group	0.60	1.05	−2.13	<.04*
14-player group	1.33	1.72	−2.29	<.03*
	Number of selections			
22-player group	0.21	0.64	−2.06	<.04*
14-player group	0.72	0.97	−1.30	>.20

*$p < .05$

General social cohesion

For the entire group, intragroup social cohesion did not evolve significantly over time: from 0.84 to 1.02, $p > .26$ (see Table 6.2). There is no significant difference in social cohesion between the first (T1) and second (T2) administrations after roughly a month of competition and following the changes made by the coaches.

For the 14 players who were there for T1 and T2, intragroup social cohesion increased significantly over time: from 1.38 to 1.69, $p < .001$.

Cohesion and position played

The players were divided into two groups according to their position on the field: from the front row to the back row they were in the forwards group, and from the scrumhalf to the fullback they were in the backs group. Due to the coaches' changes, six forwards and two backs were new in the 22-player group of T2.

The entire group

At the beginning of the competition, when the questionnaire was administered for the first time, intragroup cohesion was not significantly stronger ($t(20) = 1.95$, $p < .07$; see Table 6.3) with the backs (1.31) than with the forwards (0.83). The gap widened at the end of the competition: cohesion increased, but not significantly ($p > .32$), within the backs group (1.57) and remained stable for the forwards (0.84), leading to a significant difference ($t(20) = 2.72, p < .02$) between these two groups. So, with regard to the position played, cohesion was significantly stronger with the backs than with the forwards for the two 22-player groups, and this significant difference increased with time. These results can be explained by the changes made by the coaches: there were six new players in the group of 12 forwards, but only two new players in the group of ten backs.

Over time, the evolution of intergroup cohesion indexes is not significant (0.68 at T1, 0.91 at T2, $p > .26$) between these two subgroups – forwards and backs.

The 14-player subgroup

When the questionnaire was administered for the first time, intragroup cohesion was not significantly stronger ($t(12) = 0.81, p > .43$) for the forwards (1.80) than for the backs (1.46). Between the first and second administrations, cohesion increased to 2.33 for the forwards and 1.64 for the backs, but not significantly ($t(12) = 1.69, p > .11$).

As for the entire group, over time the increase in intergroup cohesion is not statistically significant between these two subgroups, forwards and backs (from 1.20 to 1.52, $p > .13$).

Cohesion and age

The players were divided into two groups according to their age, with a group of players 25 years and older on the one hand and on the other a group of players under 25 years. Due to the coaches' changes, the eight new players were all less than 25 years old in the 22-player group of the second administration. There were no new players in the group of players who were 25 years and older.

The entire group

At the beginning of the competition, when the questionnaire was administered for the first time, there were no significant statistical differences between the social cohesion indexes of the group of players 25 years and older and the group of players under 25 (1.21 vs. 0.95, $t(20) = 1.49, p > .15$). But for the second administration, the younger players (0.68) were significantly ($t(20) = -6.52, p < .001$) less cohesive than the older ones (2.00).

The number of days spent together did not systematically increase the subgroups' cohesion: if staying between the two reinforced cohesion between players older than 25 (from 1.21 to 2, $p < .01$), it decreased (but not statistically significantly) for younger players (from 0.95 to 0.68, $p > .11$). These results can be explained by the changes made by the coaches: the eight new players were all under 25. This means that their time together was shorter.

However, the intergroup cohesion index between these two groups increased significantly between the first time and the second time the questionnaire was administered for the 22-player group (from 0.60 to 1.05, $p < .04$) and the 14-player group (from 1.33 to 1.72, $p < .03$).

The 14-player subgroup

During the two administrations of the questionnaire, social cohesion was much stronger in the group of players who were 25 and older. The players who made it from the first administration (group 1) to the second one (group 2) showed significantly reinforced cohesion between the older players (from 1.53 to 2, $p < .01$) and lower cohesion for the under-25 group, but this was not statistically significant (from 1.26 to 1, $p > .23$). These results show that for the 14 players who stayed, cohesion was reinforced but only between players older than 25. And time had no significant impact on cohesion among younger players.

However, the cohesion index between these two groups increased significantly between the first and the second times the questionnaire was administered (from 1.33 to 1.72, $p < .03$). The intragroup index was significantly weaker than the intergroup index (1 vs. 1.72, $t(5) = -2.75$, $p < .04$), which again means that the younger players were not united whereas the older ones were, particularly at T2.

This result can also be explained by the fact that the eight new players were all young ones. At the same time, older players have the biggest number of selections: age and the number of selections are positively correlated.

Cohesion and the number of selections

The players were divided into two groups: one that was made up of those who had 12 selections and more, the other one with players who had fewer than 12. Due to the coaches' changes, the eight new players had fewer than 12 selections in the 22-player group of the second questionnaire administration.

The entire group

When the questionnaire was administered for the first time, intragroup cohesion was the same in the two groups (1.43 and 1.42), regardless of whether they had more or fewer than 12 selections ($t(20) = 0.04$, $p > .97$). Regarding the second administration, passing from group 1 to group 2 significantly reinforced cohesion between players with more than 12 selections (from 1.43 to 2.4, $p < .001$) and significantly decreased cohesion between players with fewer selections (from 1.42 to 0.77, $p < .02$). Passing from group 1 to group 2 led to a significant difference in cohesion between these two groups.

At the same time, cohesion between the two groups was very weak: the number of selections is the variable that had the lowest intergroup index (0.21). Number of selections creates the biggest division. Cohesion between the two groups increased significantly (from 0.21 to 0.64, $p < .04$), but with an intergroup index weaker than the intragroup indexes.

The 14-player subgroup

Out of these 14 players, only four had fewer than 12 selections, so the groups were very unbalanced – four to ten.

During the two questionnaire administrations, cohesion grew significantly stronger in the group of players who had 12 selections or more (from 2.08 to 2.4, $p < .01$) and weaker but not statistically significantly in that of players with fewer selections (from 0.50 to 1.16, $p > .06$). Ultimately this 14-player group was pretty tightly knit as a whole, and its intergroup cohesion was reinforced, but not significantly, the second time the questionnaire was administered (from 0.72 to 0.97, $p > .2$).

The number of selections is the strongest criterion for division of the group in two subgroups.

Discussion

The purpose of this study was to examine the evolution over time of social cohesion in the French women's national rugby union team. There are theoretical and practical implications that we can put forward.

We can highlight five general issues. Firstly, hypothesis one is validated: intragroup social cohesion evolved positively between the beginning (T1) and the end (T2) of the competition for the group of 14 players who took part in the competition from the beginning to the end. Cohesion changes over time during a group's creation and development processes (Buton et al., 2006; Carron & Brawley, 2000). In our study, it evolved in a positive way as the group matured over time (Wekselberg et al., 1997). Our analysis also shows that social cohesion either does not change or evolves positively between the beginning and the end of the competition when we look at the subgroups according to the players' position, age and number of selections. The team's stability, understood as the length of time the players remain together, is a factor that contributes to improving cohesion (Carron, 1980). The longer a team stays together, the more it gets a chance to develop its social cohesion. This is more than confirmed for the 14 players who took part in the whole competition. This result is contrary to that of Chang and Bordia (2001), who found that social cohesion showed no significant change over time. It also contradicts the results of Heuzé et al. (2006, 2007) and Leo Marcos et al. (2012), who showed that cohesion decreased over a sport season. But one major difference with these studies is the duration of the research in itself. Our study lasted only six weeks, whereas Heuzé et al. (2006, 2007) and Leo Marcos et al. (2012) studied an entire sport season.

Secondly, factors other than time can explain the increase in the group's social cohesion, such as the wins accumulated by the team. It so happens that the team did not lose a single match during the time the competition – and the study – lasted. According to Carron et al. (2002), cohesion serves as a catalyst helping with coordination in sports that are said to be collective, in which player interaction is vital to winning a match. Even if the relationship between cohesion and performance is much more circular than linear (Buton et al., 2006), a team that wins tends to see its level of agreement increase, and reciprocally, a team that is closely knit from the start is in a better condition to succeed (Carron et al., 2002; Jackson, 2011; Kozub & McDonnell, 2000; Mullen & Copper, 1994; Williams & Widmeyer, 1991). Conversely, many successive losses tend to deteriorate agreement within a group.

Thirdly, our study provides no statistical evidence of a relationship between the position played and each of these subgroups' cohesion. Yet traditionally, backs and forwards have long been part of two subgroups that are not very open to each other. Pociello (1983) detailed the antagonism between "trench rugby" – the forwards' man-to-man combat – and "champagne rugby" – the backs' evasive style of play. These representations often lead to the idea of two subgroups. On the one hand, a very socially related forward group with good social cohesion is required for man-to-man combat. On the other hand, for the backs, a less socially cohesive group is linked to their evasive style of play. This antagonism seems outdated today, at least with regard to our research.

Fourthly, our second hypothesis is also validated. The number of selections is a more significant criterion than age (Jacob & Carron, 1998) or position played for division of the group into two subgroups. The results shed light on a significant opposition between the players at a more advanced stage in their careers – with the most selections – and the younger ones. It is possible that those at a more advanced stage seek to convert their number of selections into prestige and respect for seniority.

Lastly, the fact that time increases differences in cohesion between subgroups with regard to age was not expected and could seem to contradict our first hypothesis. This result shows that time can positively increase social cohesion for the group taken as a whole and for the subgroups, but it can also highlight differences in social cohesion between these same subgroups.

Considering this survey's results, practical information emerges for coaches of elite sports teams. Thus, it would seem that (1) it is important to consider the integration of new players in sports teams and that (2) the need to be very cohesive on the field (task cohesion) does not automatically translate into social cohesiveness off the field: in rugby, the forwards are apparently not systematically more socially cohesive than the backs.

Further research should investigate the four dimensions of cohesion through the use of the Group Environment Questionnaire (Carron et al., 1985) along with the Group Conflict Questionnaire (Paradis et al., 2014).

In addition, the composition of the French team was altered during the competition. Due to the trainers' changes, only 14 players stayed in the team from the beginning to the end of the tournament; eight played only the first two games and eight others played only the last three. These changes in the team reveal one of the biggest difficulties researchers are confronted with when studying cohesiveness over time in a sports team. While there is consensus to claim that groups are dynamic entities, the temporal evolution of cohesion has rarely been studied (Carless, 2000), likely because of the difficulties and cost it entails (Anderson, 1961; Buton et al., 2006; Chang & Bordia, 2001; Terborg et al., 1976).

Conclusion

Our aim was to examine the evolution over time – a six-week tournament – of social cohesion in the French women's national rugby union team. The results show that time can have positive (1) and negative (2, 3) effects on social cohesion: (1) the more players stay together, the more the social cohesion between them evolves positively; (2) differences in the social cohesion of the subgroups constituted with regard to the players' ages increase with time; and lastly, (3) the number of selections is the most excluding criterion – more than age or position played – between players (i.e., generating the strongest separation of the group into two subgroups).

Our findings lead to major research questions. Are our results linked to the level of practice (i.e., the elite level)? Or are they influenced by the fact that all the games played during the research period ended in a win? Would we have found different results within a men's team? With other coaches?

In another sport? In order to answer these questions, new research should be undertaken in different sports, at the amateur as well as the elite level.

Acknowledgements

We wish to thank the staff of the French women's rugby union team, the 30 players who were selected to represent France and Julien Piscione (Research Cell at the French rugby federation).

References

Anderson, N.H. (1961). Group performance in an anagram task. *Journal of Social Psychology*, 55, 67–75.
Back, K.W. (1951). Influence through social communication. *Journal of Abnormal and Social Psychology*, 46, 9–22.
Bandura, A. (1977). Self-efficacy: Toward a unifying theory of behavioral change. *Psychological Review*, 84(2), 191–215.
Bollen, K., & Hoyle, R.H. (1990). Perceived cohesiveness: A conceptual and empirical examination. *Social Forces*, 69, 479–504.
Buton, F., Fontayne, P., & Heuzé, J.P. (2006). La cohésion des groupes sportifs: évolutions conceptuelles, mesures et relations avec la performance. *Movement & Sport Sciences*, 59, 9–45.
Carless, S. (2000). Reply to Carron and Brawley. *Small Group Research*, 31, 107–118.
Carron, A.V. (1980). *Social Psychology of Sport*. Ithaca, NY: Movement.
Carron, A.V., & Brawley, L.R. (2000). Cohesion: Conceptual and measurement issues. *Small Group Research*, 31, 89–106.
Carron, A.V., Brawley, L.R., & Widmeyer, W.N. (1998). The measurement of cohesiveness in sport groups. In J.L. Duda (ed.), *Advances in Sport and Exercise Psychology Measurement*. Morgantown, WV: Fitness Information Technology, pp. 213–226.
Carron, A.V., & Chelladurai, P. (1981). Cohesiveness as a factor in sport performance. *International Review of Sport Sociology*, 16, 2–41.
Carron, A.V., Colman, M.M., & Wheeler, J. (2002). Cohesion and performance in sports: A meta analysis. *Journal of Sport and Exercise Psychology*, 24, 168–188.
Carron, A.V., & Eys, M.A. (2012). *Group Dynamics in Sport*, 4th ed. Morgantown, WV: Fitness Information Technology.
Carron, A.V., Widmeyer, W.N., & Brawley, L.R. (1985). The development of an instrument to assess cohesion in sport teams: The group environment questionnaire. *Journal of Sport Psychology*, 7, 244–266.
Chang, A., & Bordia, P. (2001). A multidimensional approach to the group cohesion-group performance relationship. *Small Group Research*, 32(4), 379–405.

Cota, A.A., Evans, C.R., Dion, R.S., Kilik, L., & Longman, R.S. (1995). The structure of group cohesion. *Personality and Social Psychology Bulletin*, 21, 572–580.
Deep, S.D., Bass, B.M., & Vaughan, J.A. (1967). Some effects on business gaming of previous quasi-t group affiliations. *Journal of Applied Psychology*, 51, 426–431.
Festinger, L., Schachter, S., & Back, K. (1950). *Social Pressures in Informal Groups: A Study of a Housing Project*. New York: Harper and Bros.
Heuzé, J.P., Bosselut, G., & Thomas, J.P. (2007). Should the coaches of elite female handball teams focus on collective efficacy or group cohesion? *Sport Psychology*, 21, 383–399.
Heuzé, J.P., Sarrazin, P., Masiero, M., Raimbault, R., & Thomas, J.P. (2006). The relationships of perceived motivational climate to cohesion and collective efficacy in elite female teams. *Journal of Applied Sport Psychology*, 18(3), 201–218.
Hogg, M.A., & Hardie, E.A. (1991). Social attraction, personal attraction, and self-categorization: A field study. *Personality and Social Psychological Bulletin*, 17, 175–180.
Jackson, J.W. (2011). Reactions to a social dilemma as a function of intragroup interactions and group performance. *Group Processes and Intergroup Relations*, 15(4), 559–574.
Jacob, S., & Carron, A. (1998). The association between status and cohesion in sport teams. *Journal of Sports Sciences*, 16(2), 187–198.
Joncheray, H., Laporte, R., & Maillot, P. (2016). La cohésion sociale dans un sport collectif. L'équipe de France féminine de rugby à XV. *Jurisport*, 162, 7–9.
Kozub, S.A., & McDonnell, J.F. (2000). Exploring the relationship between cohesion and collective efficacy in rugby teams. *Journal of Sport Behavior*, 23, 120–129.
Leo, F.M., González-Ponceb, I., Sánchez-Miguela, P.A., Ivarssonc, A., & García-Calvob, T. (2015). Role ambiguity, role conflict, team conflict, cohesion and collective efficacy in sport teams: A multilevel analysis. *Psychology of Sport and Exercise*, 20, 60–66.
Leo Marcos, F.M., Sanchez-Miguel, P.-A., Sanchez-Olivia, D., Amado Alonso, D., & Garcia-Calvo, T. (2012). Evolution of perceived cohesion and efficacy over the season and their relation to success expectations in soccer teams. *Journal of Human Kinetics*, 34, 129–138.
Lott, A.J., & Lott, B.E. (1965). Group cohesiveness as interpersonal attraction: A review of relationships with antecedent and consequent variables. *Psychological Bulletin*, 64, 259–309.
Mikalachki, A. (1969). *Group Cohesion Reconsidered a Study of Blue Collar Work Groups*. London: School of Business Administration.
Moreno, J.L. (1934). *Who Shall Survive: A New Approach to the Problem of Human Interrelations*. Washington, DC: Nervous and Mental Disease Publishing Co.
Mullen, B., & Copper, C. (1994). The relation between group cohesiveness and performance: Integration. *Psychological Bulletin*, 115(2), 210–227.
Paradis, K., Carron, A., & Martin, L. (2014). Development and validation of an inventory to assess conflict in sport teams: The Group Conflict Questionnaire. *Journal of Sports Sciences*, 32(20), 1966–1978.

Pociello, C. (1983). *Sports et société, approche socio-culturelle des pratiques*. Paris: Maloine.
Randsley de Moura, G., Leader, T., Pelletier, J., & Abrams, D. (2008). Prospects for group processes and intergroup relations research: A review of 70 years' progress. *Group Processes & Intergroup Relations*, 11(4), 575–596.
Schachter, S. (1951). Deviation, rejection, and communication. *The Journal of Abnormal and Social Psychology*, 46(2), 190–207. https://doi.org/10.1037/h0062326.
Schachter, S., Ellertson, N., Mc Bride, D., & Gregory, D. (1951). An experimental study of cohesiveness and productivity. *Human Relations*, 4(4), 299–338.
Spink, K.S. (1992). Group cohesion and starting status in successful and less successful elite volleyball teams. *Journal of Sport Sciences*, 10(4), 379–388.
Steiner, I.D. (1972). *Group Process and Productivity*. New York: Academic Press.
Stevenson, M., & Durand-Bush, N. (1999). The relationship between development of a university football team and cohesion over a season. *Avante*, 5, 90–100.
Terborg, J.R., Castore, C.H., & DeNinno, J.A. (1976). *A Longitudinal Field Investigation of the Impact of Group Composition on Group Performance and Cohesion*. Technical Report, Purdue University.
Van Bergen, A., & Koelebakker, J. (1959). Group cohesiveness in laboratory experiments. *Acta Psychological*, 16, 81–98.
Wekselberg, V., Goggin, W.C., & Collings, T.J. (1997). A multifaceted concept of group maturity and its measurement and relationship to group performance. *Small Group Research*, 28(1), 3–28.
Widmeyer, W.N., Brawley, L.R., & Carron, A.V. (1985). *The Measurement of Cohesion in Sport Teams: The Group Environment Questionnaire*. London, ON: Sports Dynamics.
Williams, J.M., & Widmeyer, W.N. (1991). The cohesion-performance outcome relationship in a coacting sport. *Journal of Sport and Exercise Psychology*, 13, 364–371.
Zaccaro, S., & Lowe, C. (1988). Cohesiveness and performance: Evidence for multidimensionality. *Journal of Social Psychology*, 128, 547–558.
Zaccaro, S.J., & McCoy, M.C. (1988). The effects of task and interpersonal cohesiveness on performance of a disjunctive group task 1. *Journal of applied social psychology*, 18(10), 837–851.

Part III
Women's rugby through the eyes of others

Part III
Women's rugby through the eyes of others

7 The journey of a women's rugby coach
Passing through capillarity

Sébastien Dalgalarrondo

In this chapter, I consider the development of women's rugby in France, with a particular focus on the sport in rural areas – the "village rugby" in which new, amateur women's rugby teams are being formed, drawing on the resources at hand. I then turn to the question of how these new teams are managed and the reasons that lead male coaches to commit their energies to this new development. This reflection is based on a biographical analysis focused on the singular career of a man named Eric. This man, who is approaching 60, is devoted to rugby. He became involved in setting up a women's team in 2017 in Saint Clar, a small village in the Gers region of southwestern France that had a population of 998 in 2019. This is an extremely isolated, rural region whose economy is centred on agriculture. This region is often portrayed as one of rugby's heartlands. The club in Auch, the largest town in the Gers département, was founded in 1903. This club, the Football Club Auscitain, was one of the first rugby clubs in France, formed not long after Racing Club de France (1890), Stade Français (1892), FC Grenoble (1892) and Lyon Olympique Universitaire (1896). The inclusion of the word "football" in the club name testifies to how far it goes back. I emphasise this long history in order to highlight the very specific context of Gers. For many generations of Gers men, rugby was key to the development of masculinity. In Gers the issue of manliness, of masculinity, is closely bound to the values associated with rugby union. From this point of view, Eric is a product of this process of masculinisation through rugby. And when women's rugby began to emerge in France during the 1980s, he was one of those who asserted that rugby was not made for women. He has now been the coach of the women's team in his village for two years, and his career and his life journey thus offer an opportunity for close examination of the social mechanisms at work in such a personal U-turn.

Thick description: a biographical approach

In this chapter, I endeavour to approach what is usually described, in the anthropological tradition, as "thick description" (Denzin, 1989; Geertz, 1973). In order to do so, I draw on my long-term and close relationship with Eric. Eric is my older brother, ten years my senior. I am thus in a position, to use Ryle's image (1971), to interpret his smallest blink, and vice versa. This kind of research relationship obviously has its limitations, which have been described extensively in the literature (Bourdieu, 1987), but it also offers the opportunity for a particularly rich hermeneutic analysis, thanks primarily to the fact that in our family the conversational economy centres overwhelmingly on the subject of rugby. We are a typical rugby family, in which the three children, all boys, played rugby throughout their youth, while secretly dreaming of one day being called up for the French team, playing in the final of the national championships, etc. Thus, by virtue of my very proximity to the subject and the material on which I draw, this biographical approach necessarily runs alongside an autobiographical reflection. Like Eric, I have also changed my opinion on women's rugby, and this shift has in part been fed by my brother's experience and thinking. Finally, my decision in 2009 to choose professional rugby as a field of sociological research (Dalgalarrondo, 2015, 2018), within the more general framework of anthropology of the optimal man and contemporary processes of self-optimisation (Dalgalarrondo & Fournier, 2019), has contributed to nourishing and deepening this long and intense family conversation about rugby and how it has changed over time. This analysis, then, is built on of all of this biographical density and these hundreds of hours of communication and exchange within the family.

Passing: the issue of self-transformation

How is Eric's shift in position to be understood? His journey might be compared to a process of conversion (Darmon, 2011), but to do so would be to commit the serious error of reifying an imagined "before" and "after" and to place too much emphasis on the idea of a turning point separating two distinct phases of life. It seems to me that, on the contrary, Eric's journey should be analysed from the perspective of continuity. This is why I draw on the concept of "passing," which has found particular traction in research on aspects of race and gender (Brubaker, 2018; Allyson, 2014; O'Toole, 2002). Thinking in terms of passing makes it possible to analyse what is at play in biographical continuity, self-transformation and the social mechanisms at work in this process.

Identification and critique: the dynamics of passing

Born in 1961, Eric began playing rugby at the age of ten in the Paris region, having previously practised judo. It was in that very year, 1971, that the first mention of women's rugby appeared in the national newspaper *Le Monde*. In an article titled "A Sunday in July in Arcachon," Michel Castaing (the paper's sports correspondent from 1967 to 1975) detailed the sports activities taking place in Arcachon, a town on the southwest coast of France, in July 1971. "Arcachon's summer programme includes two events of widely divergent levels of interest," wrote Castaing,

> an international tennis tournament involving a number of well-known players and . . . a women's rugby match. Those who seek to promote the seaside resort as "a brand favoured by sophisticated people of good taste" take a dim view of this latter initiative. For once nobody will blame lazy husbands for heading off to lie on the beach on match day, while the ladies on the pitch play at "liberating" themselves a little more.
> (Le Monde, 1971, p.13)

In 1971 women's rugby was seen as being "in bad taste" and aroused genuine disgust, to use Bourdieu's categories (1984). It was to be nearly ten years before the women's rugby championship was reluctantly recognised by the French Rugby Federation (FFR) in 1979. In a 1981 article, again in *Le Monde*, this historic victory for women's rugby in France was described as a struggle against the "sexism" of the FFR, as embodied by its "president-king, Albert Ferrasse." In France as in other countries, this institutional recognition of women's rugby had only a marginal effect on the sexist culture of rugby. As sociological studies have shown (Joncheray & Tlili, 2013; Joncheray et al., 2016), rugby has been and remains one of the keys to the development of the optimal man, of the virile warrior[1] and ultimately of masculine hegemony:

> The values traditionally associated with most sports are nearly synonymous with that of being a "man." Competitiveness, strength, aggressiveness, instrumentality, and often violence not only are values central to sports but also are qualities associated with contemporary notions of masculinity. . . . While an endless array of sporting events have in their creation and practice been demonstrated to support masculine hegemony. . ., rugby football would have to be considered a quintessential example of these types of sporting practices.
> (Schacht, 1996, pp. 550–551)

This very particular masculine culture is articulated around three rituals: "survival of the fittest," "no pain, no gain" and "relational rejection of the feminine." Anne Saouter's ethnographic study, published during the same period (2000), shows that in France too, even as a new millennium was being celebrated, rugby remained men's business. In this testosterone-saturated world, women were usually reduced to the figure of "mother" or "whore" in a process of categorisation that demarcated the boundary between women and rugby. Nevertheless, despite this hostile atmosphere, the French authorities recognised women's rugby as "high-level sport" in 2000. It was in this context of rejection of women's rugby that Eric's rugby career unfolded. In 2000 he was 39, and his playing days were behind him. He had taken up coaching for amateur teams in the region. At the same time, he was volunteering at the rugby academy in Beaumont de Lomagne, a programme he had helped to revive in the early 1980s. Thus, in his own way and through his practice, Eric was also able to observe a shift in the boundaries in the late 1990s, as he saw the first girls enter the rugby academy. In the early 2010s, having coached a number of amateur clubs, received a fee on a few occasions and endured sporting disappointments, Eric decided for the first time in his life to take a break from rugby.

> I couldn't see what I was doing there any longer, money was starting to be involved, even at the low levels: I was being paid myself. It was stressful, you had to get results. I can't really explain but I'd maxed out, I didn't feel comfortable in that kind of rugby any more. Over just a few months I dropped everything, coaching and the academy. I took up cycling and started to learn the saxophone, so I could join the local country brass band I've been playing in ever since.
>
> (Eric, interview, 2019)

Yet in 2017, against all expectations, he decided to put his boots back on and return to coaching. But this time, and for the first time in his career, it was for a women's team, in the village of Saint Clar where he lives.

> To begin with I agreed to come and help out a bit, and then the coaches they had left, so I took over. Especially because some of the women on the team were girls I had taught in the Beaumont de Lomagne rugby academy. We started from nothing, the first year it was difficult to get 15 players together, we didn't win a single match. This year it's going a lot better. We've just scored our first try. You see, we've still got a long way to go! This year I've got a player who's just started playing sport,

she's 38 and she's starting with rugby! This year we started by revising the rules. So, we were all on the same page.

(Eric, interview, 2019)

Evidently, Eric's return to the role of coach was not driven by ambition for results or the frenzy of competition. What is expressed in this decision is his passion for passing on his knowledge. The pleasure of helping the group to progress, of introducing people to the game of rugby, is clearly more important to him than the competitive aspect. For Eric, women's rugby in the village is like a laboratory, where he glimpses the possibility of creating a different kind of game, starting right from the basics. This "return to its roots" aspect of women's rugby allows Eric to make full use of his experience, his skills and his knowledge. For example, he draws on his network to invite professional male players or female internationals to some training sessions – a significant illustration of the particular social dynamic at work in this process of rugby innovation. Everything remains to be done, but everything seems possible!

These interconnected historical milestones help to clarify the cultural context in which Eric's attitude changed. In the late 1990s, as men's rugby union became a professional sport, women's rugby was struggling to develop in an environment of overwhelming hostility and contempt. Women's rugby was a fringe sport, with fewer than 3,000 licensed female players in 2000.[2] Nevertheless, the beginnings had been established.

On the basis of Eric's career history, I will next explore two aspects of this emancipatory dynamic: a process of identification and a political-aesthetic attitude towards professional rugby.

Identification: Eric as trainer

Eric has been a rugby trainer for over 30 years. He began at the age of 17, when I was playing at the under-12 level, and he was my trainer. It was at this time that our intensely focused dialogue around rugby began. I was learning to tackle, to run, to conquer my fear and to pass to my teammates, and my brother was my model.

> What's interesting when you're a trainer is that you can follow the same generation through several years. You take them as under-10s and you're with them until they're under-16s, that's interesting, especially when you get a good year group. You create some great relationships, and you can see what you've passed on. You do feel proud. And then afterwards, the kids don't forget you!
>
> (Eric, interview, 2019)

Eric, who is not married and does not have children, has always taken great pleasure in passing on his knowledge and supporting young people in acquiring the physical skills specific to rugby. His early training in judo made him particularly sensitive to the issue of bodily integrity and respect for the opponent's body. This has helped him develop a sort of empathy that enables him to support young people in overcoming the fear aroused by the idea of physical confrontation. But if his career as trainer is a source of deep pride for him, this is also because, over the course of this long journey, he has had the opportunity to participate in the development of exceptional athletes. He is one of those unseen teachers who, working passionately but quietly behind the scenes, shapes "great players of the future." One of these athletes, probably the one Eric is most proud of, is Audrey Forlani, a pioneer of women's rugby in France. She began playing rugby in 1997, at the age of six, at the Beaumont de Lomagne rugby academy. Eric, along with others, was one of her trainers up to the under-14 level. She continued her training in the Toulouse region, but they remained in close contact. A few years later, Audrey Forlani had become a key figure in the French women's national team. At the time of this writing (2019), she has been capped over 20 times for France and was one of the first 24 female rugby union players in France to sign a (part-time) federal contract.[3] The many references to Forlani in our rugby conversations over the last ten years chart Eric's gradual opening to the potential of a women's rugby game. This process of adoption occurred through a phenomenon of identification.

> You could see right from the start that she was exceptional. She is rugby, she lives rugby, she's totally dedicated. But make no mistake, she doesn't just go at it with brute force, you've seen her yourself, she keeps the ball alive, she can pass and she can also get down low to tackle. She's a really good player, a complete player, with an incredible mental attitude. Honestly, it's beautiful to see what the women are doing in the French 15, in rugby sevens: women's sevens is also really beautiful. These days, I get more pleasure watching the French girls' team than the boys'.
>
> (Eric, interview, 2019)

Eric's adoption of women's rugby came through proximity and through practice. Bringing Audrey, and later other girls, into the rugby academy meant adapting facilities, developing strategies for integrating the girls, finding ways to normalise the situation so that they were treated as equals, etc. – a series of concrete actions and opportunities that enabled him to get to know the practice of women's rugby, to reevaluate his attitudes and expectations and to engage in an unspoken process of reflection. In bringing in these girls, Eric embarked on a process of self-transformation. In participating, at his own level, in a new form of rugby excellence, Eric made women's rugby his own. This rugby is all the more legitimate in his eyes because he can now claim to have contributed actively to its development.

From a critique of professionalism to the values of amateurism in the women's game

Although Eric has always been very attached to the combat aspect of rugby union, especially the crucial phase of tackling, he also loves passing and swerving. He was very quick to point out to me that the professionalisation of rugby had had the negative effect of reinforcing teams' defensive capabilities, thus "killing the game." He also repeatedly alerted me, from the early 2000s, to the danger of collisions, which sports TV channels were constantly rebroadcasting at the time.

> I'm always telling them: "why go straight into a crash if you've got a teammate alongside, you need to pass!" That's what rugby is, passing to your teammate, taking advantage of outnumbering them. It's not about breaking down your opponent. But in that way, pro rugby gives a really reductive, really physical image of rugby. If you're stronger you crash into them . . . you see it every Sunday. To my mind that's not good rugby, it's just a fight. There's no game anymore, and it's dangerous!
>
> (Eric, interview, 2019)

When I began my research into the professionalisation of rugby in France in 2009, the risk of concussion was just beginning to be raised. In the eyes of many former players like Eric, this new risk exactly embodied the way rugby had drifted and its transformation into a dangerous sporting spectacle. Rugby had become a "massacre game" (L'Équipe, 2014), a gladiatorial combat played out on AstroTurf.

> I'm really not interested in the Top 14 anymore, I don't watch it as often as I used to, it's too much of a stereotype of rugby, constant collisions, the forwards are in danger. It's not good to watch, and frankly, these young players are taking huge risks, what's happening with concussion is serious! We need to get back to a rugby where all bodies can express themselves, where you respect your opponent and their body. Money has a lot to answer for.
>
> (Eric, interview, 2019)

Our discussions around rugby during the 2010s were marked by this rise in violence in men's rugby. This critique of professionalisation and the form of play it had produced led Eric to gradually lose interest in men's rugby, to the point where virtually the only matches he watched on television were women's matches. His recent career U-turn is thus closely bound up with his growing rejection of men's professional rugby. By becoming the coach of a village women's team, Eric is taking the opportunity to return to the roots of amateur rugby.

> Yeah, I accepted because to me it's really interesting to start from zero, to build something. We haven't had much funding, we're still a bit isolated, but the girls have loads of energy and enthusiasm, so it's a pleasure to help them. It's going back to the roots, it really is! Tiny changing rooms, mud. Here everyone is welcome, we're far from the elite, but probably closer to the values of rugby. I'm enjoying sharing again, enjoying amateurism! It's hard to manage the different levels in the group, but that's also really stimulating. You have to work so that all the girls, whether they're beginners or more advanced, find their place and enjoy it.
>
> (Eric, interview, 2019)

Eric has put his critique into practice. He is reconnecting with the practice of village rugby, which above and beyond the pleasure of the game has the added benefits of creating social bonds, weaving networks of friendship and encouraging respect for diversity.

Conclusion: passing through capillarity

The radical shift in Eric's attitude towards women's rugby can be explained in terms of (1) a process of identification and (2) a critique of professional rugby. Considered analytically, Eric's passing derives less from a reflection on gender and femininity than from an essentialist approach to the game of rugby. In his view, it is in amateur rugby that the true values of the sport are to be found – a rugby that values the diversity of bodies and of physical and tactical skills, in which each player can find their place, complementing one another in a synergistic whole. One story to which our family frequently returns offers a perfect example of this kind of inclusivity in rugby. At Beaumont de Lomagne, a young man with mild learning disabilities had for many years the job of posting the score during official matches. Local legend even has it that he learned to count at the stadium. His occasional errors regularly reminded supporters of his presence, his consistency and his deep attachment to the club. Known to everyone, Hubert was fully part of the club with a role to play every Sunday, indirectly becoming part of the game and the club's history despite the fact that he did not play. It was Eric's attachment to values like these that led him gradually, little by little, to move from a position of rejecting women's rugby to that of fervently advocating it. Eric's U-turn thus emerged through a process of change by "capillarity" (Foucault, 2001) – a capillarity that matches the grain of day-to-day life and his everyday actions and decisions, a practical process of apprenticeship, adoption and familiarisation through contact with his neighbours and with other ways of living (Macé, 2016). From this point of view, the entry of the first girls into the rugby academy was a seminal experience in Eric's life and also underlines the importance of these pioneers. By demonstrating a way of life that challenged the status quo, these young women and their parents helped to normalise women's rugby from the bottom up.

I end by turning to the issue inherent in any phenomenon of passing – that of dissimulation. In this case, it would be more correct to think in terms of "secrecy." When I talked with female players trained by Eric, I realised that they knew nothing of his past views. His current commitment seems to speak for him: he has become a true "incarnation" (Hauray & Dalgalarrondo, 2019) of women's rugby and its values. In the everyday, friendly sociability of this very young team, concrete action prevails over long speeches. Day after day, training session after training session, defeat after defeat, Eric speaks his truth about women's rugby, and the strength of his day-to-day commitment seems to render any questioning of the consistency of his life journey superfluous.

Notes

1 See, for example, the many promotional images portraying male rugby players in the Top 14 (the top level of men's rugby in France) as Roman gladiators.
2 Rugby players in France are licensed by the FFR via affiliated clubs.
3 A professional contract with the national rugby federation issued to professional female rugby union players in France.

References

Allyson, H. (2014). *A Chosen Exile: A History of Racial Passing in American Life*. Cambridge: Harvard University Press.
Bourdieu, P. (1984). *Distinction: A Social Critique of the Judgment of Taste*, trans. by Richard Nice. Cambridge: Harvard University Press.
Bourdieu, P. (1987). The biographical illusion. *Working Papers and Proceedings of the Centre for Psychosocial Studies*, 14, 1–7.
Brubaker, R. (2018). *Trans: Gender and Race in an Age of Unsettled Identities*. Princeton: Princeton University Press.

Dalgalarrondo, S. (2015). Les dispositifs de prise de risques dans le rugby professionnel. *Sociologie du Travail*, 57, 516–535.

Dalgalarrondo, S. (2018). Surveiller et guérir le corps optimal: Big Data et performance sportive. *L'Homme et la Société*, 207(2), 99–116.

Dalgalarrondo, S., & Fournier, T. (2019). Optimization as morality, or the routes of the self. *Ethnologie Française*, 176(4), 639–651.

Darmon, M. (2011). Sociologie de la conversion. Socialisation et transformations individuelles. In C. Burton-Jeangros & C. Maeder (eds.), *Identité et transformation des modes de vie*. Geneva and Zurich: Seismo, pp. 64–84.

Denzin, N.K. (1989). *Interpretive Interactionism*. Newbury Park, CA: Sage.

Foucault, M. (2001). Le jeu de Michel Foucault, Ornicar? Bulletin périodique du champ freudien, 10, juillet 1977. In M. Foucault (ed.), *Dits et écrits II, 1976–1988*, vol. 206. Paris: Quarto Gallimard, pp. 298–329.

Geertz, C. (1973). *The Interpretation of Cultures: Selected Essays*. New York: Basic Books.

Hauray, B., & Dalgalarrondo, S. (2019). Incarnation and the dynamics of medical promises: DHEA as a fountain of youth hormone. *Health*, 23(6), 639–655.

Joncheray, H., Level, M., & Richard, R. (2016). Identity socialization and construction within the French national rugby union women's team. *International Review for the Sociology of Sport*, 51(2), 162–177.

Joncheray, H., & Tlili, H. (2013). Are there still social barriers to women's rugby? *Sport in Society*, 16(6), 772–788.

Le Monde, (1971). "Un Dimanche à Arcachon," p. 13.

L'Équipe (2014, December 7). Rugby jeu de massacre? https://www.lequipe.fr/explore/lf04-rugby-jeu-de-massacre/ [Accessed March 18, 2021].

Macé, M. (2016). *Styles. Critique de nos formes de vie*. Paris: Gallimard.

O'Toole, J.M. (2002). *Passing for White: Race, Religion, and the Healy Family, 1820–1920*. Amherst: University of Massachusetts Press.

Ryle, G. (1971). *Collected Papers, Volume II: Collected Essays, 1929–1968*. London: Hutchinson.

Saouter, A. (2000). "*Être rugby*": *jeux du masculin et du féminin*. Paris: Éditions de la Maison des sciences de l'homme.

Schacht, S. (1996). Misogyny on and off the "pitch": The gendered world of male rugby players. *Gender and Society*, 10(5), 550–565.

8 Women's experiences of rugby culture in Aotearoa/ New Zealand

Naked women talk about sport

Amy Wallace, Steve Jackson and Marcelle C. Dawson

Rugby in New Zealand has recently been the subject of a number of high-profile scandals that have tarnished the national sport and particular athletes and teams. In 2016, an incident popularly referred to as "Stripper-gate" occurred, involving players from the Waikato Chiefs Super rugby team. The Chiefs players were part of an end-of-season party at the Okoroire Hot Springs Hotel where there was heavy drinking and an incident of homophobia (Malone et al., 2016). In addition, a stripper (exotic dancer) who had been invited to perform at the event later alleged that she had been touched inappropriately and that alcohol and gravel were thrown at her (Malone et al., 2016). The story became the focus of media attention, eventually encompassing players, teams, sponsors, New Zealand Rugby (NZR), members of the public, a range of social agencies and even politicians (Trevett, 2016). In response, New Zealand Rugby undertook a formal review process that included independent witnesses. Making matters worse, only a few months later, All Black halfback Aaron Smith was involved in what became known as "Toilet-gate." Smith was caught going into a public toilet with a woman at Christchurch airport just prior to the All Blacks departure for a test match in South Africa. Members of the public reported the tryst, with the news reaching All Blacks management in South Africa the next day. After confirming the validity of the facts with Smith, it was agreed that he would return to New Zealand both as a punishment and to allow him to deal with personal matters (Otago Daily Times, October 6, 2016). In combination, Stripper-gate and Toilet-gate were major public relations disasters for New Zealand Rugby that brought the issue of rugby culture under the national microscope. In response, New Zealand Rugby established the Respect and Responsibility Review (RRR), which delivered a range of recommendations. For some New Zealanders, the review was a positive sign that the NZR was being proactive in addressing a serious issue. However, for others, Stripper-gate and Toilet-gate were just the latest in a long list of incidents that reflect a serious crisis with the culture of the national game and NZR's failure to acknowledge its problem and undertake meaningful change.

Rugby culture and gender relations in New Zealand

Rugby has long been a defining feature of New Zealand's culture and national identity (Nauright & Chandler, 1996; Phillips, 1987, 1996; Scherer & Jackson, 2010, 2013). While the sport is admittedly no longer the sole focus of the national imaginary, it remains popular among the population. Notably, while male participation has declined slightly over the last decade, the number of female players has doubled since 2012 to almost 28,000, which is about 20% of all rugby players in New Zealand (New Zealand Herald, September 19, 2018). Moreover, increasing attention has been paid to the place of women *in* the sport, with a particular focus on barriers to participation and leadership roles, inequities in funding and issues related to media representation.

However, to date, there has been limited research on women's experiences *with* rugby and its subculture. Indeed, there is scant literature about women who do not play a particular sport themselves but have relationships with men who do. For example, we know little about the experiences of women as girlfriends, partners, wives, sisters and mothers, who support sport and the men in their lives who play it. While some women have had positive experiences, there is also evidence to suggest negative experiences related to (1) lack of recognition of their personal sacrifices and their own interests in either playing or watching sport (Gmelch & San Antonio, 2001; Pope, 2013); (2) lack of recognition of their emotional and other support, including domestic tasks (Clayton & Harris, 2004; Ortiz, 2011; O'Toole, 2006; Thompson, 1999); (3) issues of sexuality and sexual stereotypes (Bruce, 2013; Ezzell, 2009; Joncheray, 2013; Saouter, 1995; Wright & Clarke, 1999), such as being referred to as "WAGS" (wives and girlfriends or "groupies"); and (4) safety related to harassment, alcohol consumption and the hypermasculine context of sports (Card & Dahl, 2011; Crossett, 1999; Dunning, 1986; Gee & Jackson, 2017; Messner, 1990, 2002; Messner & Sabo, 1994; Muir & Seitz, 2004; Nauright & Chandler, 1996; Pringle, 2004; Robinson, 1998; Saouter, 2014; Schacht, 1996; Sheard & Dunning, 1973; Thompson, 1988).

This chapter is part of a larger study of women's experiences with sport and focuses on the connection between rugby, its subculture and the experiences of a select group of women who are partners of male rugby players. Drawing upon a series of interviews, we examine how women experience rugby culture, giving priority to their voices as they talk about their lives as partners of rugby players. The reference to "naked" women in the title is a metaphor used to characterise the process of women "baring their souls" about life, love and relationships with their rugby-playing partners.

Methodology

A qualitative, interpretive approach was employed in this study. Specifically, in-depth, semistructured, open-ended interviews with five individuals were undertaken with the aim of "going beyond surface understandings, to explore the contextual meanings of behaviors" (Tracy, 2019, p. 31). Our interpretations were informed by participants' own understanding of their lived experiences (Smith & Sparkes, 2016; Tracy, 2019). The five female participants involved in this study were selected by using purposeful sampling, which offers researchers access to information-rich individuals with first-hand experience (Patton, 1990). The participants included women of different ages and socioeconomic backgrounds, whose partners played rugby at varying levels: National Provincial Championship (NPC), Premier Club, Senior Club, High School and Social. Participants gave informed consent, indicating that they understood the nature of the project and their right to withdraw at any time. Audiotaped interviews were held with each participant, lasting for about an hour each. In addition, one group interview session was held involving all five participants. All interviews were transcribed verbatim and analysed in relation to emerging themes. An audit check was undertaken by a person not associated with the project to ensure both logic and accuracy of data interpretation.

Table 8.1 offers a brief profile of each participant, noting their pseudonym, age, playing level of their male partner and their overall experience with and attitude towards rugby, rated in relation to positive, negative or neutral.

Table 8.1 Participant profiles

Name	Age	Partner's rugby level	Experience with rugby (positive, negative or neutral)
Melanie	Mid-20s	Elite	Negative
Elise	20	Premier club and provincial Māori	Neutral
Bridget	Early 20s	Senior club	Positive, but with concerns
Kay	19	Social	Positive
Lottie	17	High school	Neutral

Results and discussion

Ultimately, our aim was to offer information-rich data that represented the ideas and experiences of the women participants and that prioritised their voices. Analysis of the interview data revealed 28 raw categories, which were grouped into five general themes including (1) women's positive and negative experiences with rugby culture, (2) women's positions and roles in rugby culture, (3) boys' zones (sport as exclusive spaces of masculinity), (4) the holy trinity (sport, alcohol and masculinity) and (5) the institution of rugby. It is important to note that each of these themes is worthy of in-depth analysis but, for the purposes of this chapter, we attempted to balance breadth with depth in order to provide a more rounded presentation. Unsurprisingly, given the qualitative nature of the study, there was considerable overlap in the themes, and this is reflected in the narratives that follow. In the interests of authenticity and dynamism, we have presented the results in the form of a conversation with the participants, stating the question that was posed along with selected responses to highlight particular themes.

Overall, our analysis explores the experiences of women within the framework of the gender order (Connell, 1987, 1995), with a particular focus on the relationship between sport and hegemonic masculinity. Within the logic of the gender order, sport reproduces a dominant masculinity that not only marginalises women but also pressures some men to be complicit, by subordinating and marginalising those who do not meet the criteria or who fail to conform. Pease (2000, p. 3) noted the intended and unintended consequences of the gender order and hegemonic masculinity:

> Not all men are batterers and rapists, but without "ordinary" men's participation in routine oppressive practices, men's subordination of women would not take the form it does. Furthermore, because so many men's oppressive behaviour is socially accepted as "normal male behaviour", it can be said to impede their awareness of its oppressive aspects.

Ultimately, some sports, including rugby, continue to serve as arenas of masculinity where male power can be publicly performed, circulated and celebrated. In turn, this impacts on the lived experiences of both women and men in wider society. At this point, we examine the first category of analysis to provide a brief overview of some of the contrasting positive and negative experiences of the participants with rugby.

Women's positive and negative experiences with rugby culture

Although one focus of this chapter is on the challenges and negative effects of rugby culture on women, it would be misleading not to mention that most of our participants also acknowledged a positive side of the sport. For example, during the group interview, the issue of camaraderie within the sport emerged. Mel stated (with all the others agreeing) that rugby represents

> Brothers-in-arms. It's sort of an acceptance and acknowledgement that for 80 minutes you just played your guts out but you're still mates and they've given their all and you've given yours. That's acknowledged and [the two teams] respect it.

Elise went on to say that she believed that inclusion was another positive factor gained through involvement in rugby:

> [Rugby is] a good sport where all shapes and sizes can get involved. It's not like only big people can play. You can be a winger or you can be a tall, skinny lock. It's quite inclusive now, especially with women's rugby as well because it's not just something for guys.

She added that playing rugby was also a good way to keep fit. In turn, Kay talked about the cathartic effect that rugby provided, in that it was a way in which players could relieve stress.

Despite these positive signals about brotherhood and male bonding, inclusiveness and the increasing number of female players in the game, there was an overwhelming view that rugby and its culture had some negative aspects. For example, rugby was perceived to be quite violent, and concerns were raised about the potential of violence on the field to spread to postgame contexts. For example, Kay stated,

> I think it [violent acts on the field spilling over off the field] happens, but I think it's really wrong. They [those involved in rugby] urge you ... to win by physical play. People don't always leave what happens on the field, on the field.

She went on to add that she did not like the physical component of rugby and was concerned about the overbearing strength of rugby players. She made a point about how sometimes rugby players do not realise how strong they are, including with their female partners:

> Just being pushed around or being pushed into something [you] don't want to do. Just being knocked around if you say "no." Shoved out of the way or pushed into things.

Kay, Mel and Lottie all agreed that they did not like the attitudes of some rugby players. For example, when asked to share a story, the participants looked at each other and then Mel offered a perspective with which the others agreed:

> The drinking. The arrogance. The mongrel attitude. Just that [the rugby players] are the all and everything. You must bow down to them and treat them with respect. . . . Because rugby has been portrayed for years . . . as a real bloke's game and rugby players are to be idolised. That had just evolved through time. Now that rugby has turned professional the rugby guys think they are owed everything they get, they don't have to work for it.

Mel's statement reflected many of the stereotypes associated with rugby culture, including drinking and an aggressive group or pack mentality (mongrel attitude). Notably, she also referred to the issue of status and what, in American terms, has been described as the "big man on campus" syndrome (Melnick, 1992), where athletes develop a sense of entitlement. Moreover, Mel's observations highlight that the professionalisation of rugby has only escalated the problem. Next, we examine the experiences of the participants with respect to their positions and roles within the context of rugby culture.

Women's positions and roles in rugby culture

The participants were asked to consider their current involvement with the sport of rugby. In response, Mel indicated that,

> I guess now I'm a rugby widow. I'm abandoned every weekend and every Tuesday and Thursday night for practice. Like other partners of the NPC team I am also involved with supporting the development team. I'm sick of going along watching, which sounds awful, but the rugby drags on too long for me. It's a full year thing for me. My partner started training on the 7th of January and he's still training [September]. The NPC teams go on for another two weeks after that if they make semis and finals so that'll go on 'till the end of October. Then they get November off and then they'd be expected to start training again in December.

Here, the term "rugby widow" is used to signify the fact that her partner's sport participation impacts on the couple's social life, such that she feels alone for much of the year. The other participants agreed that they are largely sideline supporters who occasionally join their partners at postgame functions. Given that Kay actually played rugby herself, we asked if her friends and partner would go along to watch. She replied that,

> A couple of your close mates will but not everyone. If my boyfriend is playing at the same time as me, even my own friends will probably go and watch his game because he's got more mates with him.

From Kay's comments, it was not clear whether her friends' preference to watch her partner's game instead of her own was because the skill level was perceived to be higher, or because her friends were also friends with her partner's teammates, or perhaps her friends were interested in developing relationships with them. This discussion led into the next question about rugby as an exclusive space for men, often characterised as "boys' time" or "zones of masculinity," where men have time away from women, whether it be competing on the field, spending time in changing rooms or drinking and socialising at the pub or clubhouse.

Boys' zones: sport as exclusive spaces of masculinity

We asked the participants how they felt about what they had described as "boys' time." Bridget responded (with Lottie and Elise agreeing) that she did not mind her partner having his own space, as they would otherwise get sick of each other. Mel was also supportive of "boys' time," except when it became excessive.

> As far as I'm concerned training is boys' time and after the match in changing rooms is boys' time. When they go away for games, that's boys' time. It doesn't bother me, it's when it becomes excessive, like if they've just been away for three days and they've just had training and my partner wants to go out on a boys' night. I'm like, "hang on a minute, what about our time?"

Kay generally approved of her partner's time with his mates, but she did note that it had the potential to be negative when boys' talk was derogatory or demeaning towards women. With that as a prompt, the other participants also noted their reservations about men talking about "scoring" or who is "easy." Elise was not sure whether the boys "went into detail," but she did confirm that there was a lot more "filthy talk" when they had been drinking. She attributed this behaviour to group dynamics and peer pressure, because "rugby culture is tough and if you talk about girls then you're tough and macho." We followed up this discussion with questions about their experiences of postmatch functions. Lottie indicated that although she was always invited, she rarely attended because,

> they're really loud and the [players have] been drinking and I'm not a big drinker. I just don't know if I really like that sort of atmosphere – the whole big boozing up afterwards thing.

Elise agreed with Lottie and rarely attended rugby social functions for the same reasons. Bridget, Kay and Mel were all fairly neutral in their views of postmatch functions, highlighting that they knew it was part of the tradition. Indeed, Mel, whose partner played at the elite level, indicated that she was

> invited to the after matches for all of the [NPC teams'] events. The team has a fantastic environment for the partners. Every weekend when the boys are away [playing rugby], they'll organise something for the girls. Whether it's a lunch or drinks somewhere. The first home game of the season, they organise [for] the wives and the partners to go into the corporate boxes. And the manager is really good at making sure the wives and partners get tickets to the games and are included, where possible.

Thus, Mel had a positive experience within a more professionalised rugby context, but she also noted her disapproval of one particular part of the after-match functions, namely, court sessions. Court sessions are a postgame ritual where players are publicly shamed for a range of infractions, including mistakes during a game, being late for training or doing anything that violates the "male code of honour." According to Mel,

> only the boys go to court sessions and it's a time where you write yourself off as much as possible because the alcohol is free. I don't like the fact that they go out to get as drunk as they possibly can and become absolute mongrels. I don't like [it when] every game you've got to have a court session. That's really exclusive.

According to Bridget, at court sessions,

> They do really stupid things. Like they have to turn up in women's underwear or they have to wear women's togs [bathing suits] and it's all about games and having fun and building team spirit. That's what they tell us.

The topic of drinking emerged throughout the interviews regardless of the questions posed, highlighting the centrality of alcohol and what has been described as the "holy trinity," which we discuss in the next section.

The holy trinity: sport, alcohol and masculinity

The emphasis on drinking within rugby culture confirms the holy trinity of sport, beer and masculinity (Wenner & Jackson, 2009). To begin, we asked the participants about how alcohol affects their partner's behaviour. Bridget noted that, as an individual, her partner tended to drink in order to relax after work, but then described alcohol consumption in relation to rugby culture more broadly:

> The amount of drinking that they do, it's just phenomenal! Most Saturday nights they will all go back to the club and they'll have a few beers and then have a few more and things get out of hand. You can guarantee on a Saturday night that you won't really see your partner. He's out with the team. I guess you get used to that? It's a rugby thing. But then a lot of the other partners of the rugby players don't like to go out with them or get involved like that.

She continued, describing how her own partner would become arrogant, stubborn and difficult to reason with when he had been drinking. "I know he doesn't mean it. It's just [what] alcohol does to people." Elise responded (with all the others agreeing) that some rugby players "drink until they fall over" and "do disgusting things which are often praised in the rugby culture." She added that her partner "becomes more abusive" and that "alcohol seems to make him less inhibited." In response, Mel described one incident that stuck in her mind:

> There was just one night where he just wrote himself off and came home and was just an absolute disgrace. Just awful and that almost split us up. He was just aggressive, drunk and it was only because he was drunk. I put him on the couch, he sobers up and we deal with it the next day. If I've been drinking as well then we'll have a rip-roaring argument. There's no point in [talking about] it when he's been drinking. You can't have an argument with a drunk person. You can't resolve anything with a drunk person. [It's a] no win situation. When you're drunk, you say and do nasty things.

We noticed that Mel stopped talking abruptly. Concerned, we followed up the next day when she was on her own. Mel eventually opened up and shared that her partner's behaviour changed when he was drunk:

> He goes silly. He's not one of those guys that gets abusive or aggressive when he drinks. He just goes really dumb. I don't think he's affected by alcohol. . . [long pause]. Once, there was one occasion, but I've never actually seen him that drunk.

"What did he do?" we asked, trying not be too invasive. She described how he came home one night and was "really abusive and loud." When asked if he was emotionally or physically abusive, she replied, "both," and then gradually revealed that:

> He slapped me. But I know it wasn't meant. I think it was just a complete frustration that he was so drunk and I was trying to point him in the direction of the toilet and he couldn't find it. That's how drunk he was. But that's the only time he has even been abusive.

Strangely, when reminded that she had previously stated that her partner's behaviour did not really change when he had been drinking, Mel still said, "Yes, that is right, he doesn't really change." This particular interview was emotional and disturbing and unmasked the darker side of rugby culture or, more accurately, hegemonic masculine sport culture. It prompted us to reflect upon the influence of sport culture and the institutional factors that shape it. Accordingly, the next section briefly examines how the female participants experienced and perceived the institution of rugby.

The institution of rugby

In this final section, we attempt to get a sense of the institution of rugby, that is, how rugby clubs and organisations establish rules and values and, in turn, manage behaviours that contradict these values. Mel had more insider knowledge than the other participants about the role of rugby clubs and their administrators, given her partner's involvement at the elite level. When asked about the repercussions of a club player being reprimanded, Mel replied:

> They support them. They always send a club representative with a player to a judicial hearing to make sure that they can support them. If they think the guy has got issues, they take them aside and look after them. They are actually a really good club like that.

In turn, we asked, "What about the NPC, what happens if someone gets into trouble *outside of rugby*, what happens then?"

> They're really, really supportive. The team manager has his phone on 24 hours a day and a player can ring him at any time and he will go out and go and help them. It has happened because there have been guys that have got into fights at pubs and they've just rung [him] and he has gone down and got them out and takes them home. They help with the media. They have a media liaison lady and she makes sure that the media only gets the information that they need. They've got lawyers tied up with the team, just everything's there for them. They have that support network.

These responses highlight that the institution of rugby generally supports players whether their infractions occur within the game or in public. In some cases, this support takes the form of maintaining a code of silence, popularly captured in the phrase "what goes on tour, stays on tour." Here, protecting the players and maintaining the culture of the club is paramount. However, it should be noted that times have changed, and in the era of new media technologies, the surveillance capabilities within the public sphere are omnipresent. As a result, while elite rugby teams and their management have formal structures in place to manage a range of individual player indiscretions, organisations are also acutely aware of the reputational brand damage that a player's or team's actions can have. As such, support is provided to players in trouble, but where the evidence of wrongdoing is overwhelming, the institution of rugby is increasingly more likely to investigate, acknowledge the problem and not only discipline those involved but, as revealed in the cases of Stripper-gate and Toilet-gate, undertake a formal review to establish new guidelines and policies.

Conclusion

The results of this study highlight the experiences of women within the culture of New Zealand's national sport of rugby in relation to five interrelated themes, including (1) women's positive and negative experiences with rugby culture, (2) women's positions and roles in rugby culture, (3) boys' zones (sport as exclusive spaces of masculinity), (4) the holy trinity (sport, alcohol and masculinity) and (5) the institution of rugby. At first glance, particularly for some male rugby traditionalists, the results would suggest that the trials and tribulations discussed by our participants are rather mundane. However, it is arguably the "mundaneness" – the normalised and taken-for-granted nature of these women's experiences and their relationships with their partners – that is the key point. The results highlight the way in which the participants negotiated and, at times, even resisted key aspects of their relationships with their partners and rugby culture. However, by and large, whether it is undertaking domestic duties such as doing laundry, accepting boys' time at the expense of shared partner time, dealing with excessive drinking, and even coping with emotional and physical abuse, the female participants in this study remained loyal, both to their partners and to the game of rugby. Whether we wish to consider this a symptom of the gender order and how it operates in and through rugby culture is a matter for further discussion and debate.

What is clear is that recent scandals (e.g., Stripper-gate and Toilet-gate) may have been the tipping point for New Zealand Rugby with regard to its reputation and legitimacy, particularly with respect to gender relations. These scandals, combined with a number of other factors, including the significant increase in the number of female rugby players in Aotearoa/New Zealand, the ongoing success of the Black Ferns Women's National Team, a 2019 government announcement to fund and promote sport participation for girls and women, and securing the hosting rights to the 2021 Rugby World Cup (the first gender-neutral global sporting event), all likely played a role in putting pressure on the NZR to ensure that it was being proactive in developing an inclusive rugby culture for the nation. The NZR's response was to set up the Respect and Responsibility Review (RRR) (Cockburn & Atkinson, 2017a, 2017b).

The RRR panel consisted of a range of men and women from across a diverse set of social sectors, such as sport, business and the legal world, and included Kathryn Beck (Chair), Jackie Barron, Lisa Carrington, Kate Daly, Liz Dawson, David Howman, Sir Michael Jones, Keven Mealamu and Dr. Deb Robinson, with Robyn Cockburn and Lucy Atkinson serving as authors of the report. The summary report begins with the following statement:

> New Zealand Rugby's mission is to Inspire and Unify. . . . Events prior to and in 2016 began to undermine rugby's place and contribution. . . . NZ Rugby has a commitment to lead, grow, support and promote our game. These strategic aspirations are underpinned by a series of values that shape the principles and practices of the rugby community.
>
> (Cockburn & Atkinson, 2017a, p. 2)

From the outset, the report acknowledges that the 2016 scandals undermined rugby's place and contribution in New Zealand and that NZR has a responsibility to change and lead reforms. Ultimately the review concluded with six major, overarching goals for the NZR: (1) Inclusive: Inclusive

Leadership, (2) Progressive: Developing Better People, (3) Integrity: Nurturing Wellbeing, (4) Empowering: Gender Equality, (5) Respectful: Proactive Engagement and (6) World Leading: Accountable and Independent. The stated goals of the report signal a clear commitment by the NZR to change and be held accountable. However, only time and careful monitoring will reveal whether the NZR and the RRR's recommendations will be enough to save rugby's reputation and protect its future as the national sport in New Zealand. Ultimately, it is clear that in order to be successful, fundamental changes in the culture of rugby – particularly with respect to gender relations – are required.

References

Bruce, T. (2013). Reflections on communication and sport: On women and femininities. *Communication & Sport*, 1, 125–137.

Card, D., & Dahl, G.B. (2011). Family violence and football: The effect of unexpected emotional cues on violent behavior. *The Quarterly Journal of Economics*, 126(1), 103–143.

Clayton, B., & Harris, J. (2004). Footballers' wives: The role of the soccer player's partner in the construction of idealized masculinity. *Soccer and Society*, 5(3), 317–335.

Cockburn, R., & Atkinson, L. (2017a). *Respect and Responsibility Review – New Zealand Rugby: Full Report*. Wellington: Lumin. www.nzrugby.co.nz/assets/NZR-RRR-Final-Review-Report.pdf [Accessed March 17, 2021].

Cockburn, R., & Atkinson, L. (2017b). *Respect and Responsibility Review – New Zealand Rugby: Summary*. Wellington: Lumin. www.nzrugby.co.nz/assets/NZR-RRR-Summary-Document.pdf [Accessed March 17, 2021].

Connell, R.W. (1987). *Gender and Power*. Cambridge: Polity Press.

Connell, R.W. (1995). *Masculinities*. St Leonards: Allen & Unwin.

Crossett, T. (1999). Male athletes' violence against women: A critical assessment of the athletic affiliation, violence against women debate. *Quest*, 51(3), 244–257.

Dunning, E. (1986). Sport as a male preserve: Notes on the social sources of masculine identity and its transformations. *Theory, Culture & Society*, 3(1), 79–90.

Ezzell, M. (2009). 'Barbie dolls' on the pitch: Identity work, defensive othering and inequality in women's rugby. *Social Problems*, 56(1), 111–131.

Gee, S., & Jackson, S.J. (2017). *Sport, Promotional Culture and the Crisis of Masculinity*. London: Palgrave Macmillan.

Gmelch, G., & San Antonio, P.M. (2001). Baseball wives: Gender and the work of baseball. *Journal of Contemporary Ethnography*, 30(3), 335–356.

Joncheray, H., & Tlili, H. (2013). Are there still social barriers to women's rugby? *Sport in Society*, 6(6), 772–788.

Malone, A., Kerr, F., Hinton, M., Edens, J., & Robinson, G. (2016, August 4). *Stripper Speaks Out, Alleges Chiefs Players Inappropriately Touched Her, Stuff*. www.stuff.co.nz/sport/rugby/super-rugby/82789997/chiefs-in-hot-water-over-stripper-fracas [Accessed March 17, 2021].

Malone, A., Pearson, J., & van Royen, R. (2016, August 2). *Chiefs Forward Michael Allardice Admits Anti-Gay Slur at Post Season Party*. www.stuff.co.nz/sport/rugby/super-rugby/82713817/chiefs-apologise-launch-investigation-into-alleged-antigay-slur-at-post-season-party [Accessed March 17, 2021].

Melnick, M. (1992). Male athletes and sexual assault. *Journal of Physical Education, Recreation & Dance*, 63(5), 32–36.

Messner, M.A. (1990). When bodies are weapons: Masculinity and violence in sport. *International Review for the Sociology of Sport*, 25(3), 203–220.

Messner, M.A. (2002). *Taking the Field: Women, Men, and Sports*. Minneapolis: University of Minnesota Press.

Messner, M.A., & Sabo, D.F. (1994). *Sex, Violence & Power in Sports: Rethinking Masculinity*. Freedom, CA: The Crossing Press.

Muir, K.B., & Seitz, T. (2004). Machismo, misogyny, and homophobia in a male athletic subculture: A participant-observation study of deviant rituals in collegiate rugby. *Deviant Behavior*, 25(4), 303–332.

Nauright, J., & Chandler, T. (eds.) (1996). *Making Men: Rugby and Masculine Identity*. London: Frank Cass.

New Zealand Herald (2018, September 19). *Rugby: Females a Fifth of All Players*. www.nzherald.co.nz/sport/news/article.cfm?c_id=4&objectid=12127575 [Accessed March 17, 2021].

Ortiz, S.M. (2011). Wives who play by the rules: Working on emotions in the sport marriage. In A.I. Garey & K.V. Hansen (eds.), *At the Heart of Work and Family: Engaging the Ideas of Arlie Hochschild*. New Brunswick: Rutgers University Press, pp. 124–135.

Otago Daily Times (2016, October 6). *Aaron Smith on Way Home from ABs Tour*. www.odt.co.nz/sport/rugby/all-blacks/aaron-smith-sent-home-abs-tour [Accessed March 17, 2021].

O'Toole, S. (2006). *Married to the Game: The Real Lives of NFL Women*. Lincoln: University of Nebraska Press.

Patton, M. (1990). *Qualitative Evaluation and Research Methods*, 2nd ed. Newbury Park, CA: Sage.

Pease, B. (2000). *Recreating Men: Postmodern Masculinity Politics*. London: Sage.

Phillips, J. (1987). *A Man's Country? The Image of the Pakeha Male-A History*. Auckland: Penguin.

Phillips, J. (1996). The hard man: Rugby and the formation of male identity in New Zealand. In J. Nauright & T. Chandler (eds.), *Making Men: Rugby and Masculine Identity*. London: Frank Cass, pp. 70–90.

Pope, S. (2013). The love of my life: The meaning and importance of sports for female fans. *Journal of Sport & Social Issues*, 37(2), 176–195.

Pringle, R. (2004). A social-history of the articulations between rugby union and masculinities within Aotearoa/New Zealand. *New Zealand Sociology*, 19(1), 102–128.

Pringle, R. (2008). 'No rugby – no fear': Collective stories, masculinities and transformative possibilities in schools. *Sport, Education and Society*, Toronto, 13(2), 215–237.

Robinson, L. (1998). *Crossing the Line: Violence and Sexual Assault in Canada's National Sport*. Toronto: McClelland & Stewart.

Saouter, A. (1995). La maman et la putain: Les hommes, les femmes et le rugby. *Terrain: Anthropologie & Sciences Humaine*, 25, 13–24.
Saouter, A. (2014). «*Être rugby*»: *jeux du masculin et du féminin*. [E-book]. Paris: Paris Éditions de la Maison des sciences de l'homme.
Schacht, S.P. (1996). Misogyny on and off the "pitch": The gendered world of male rugby players. *Gender & Society*, 10(5), 550–565.
Scherer, J., & Jackson, S.J. (2010). *Sport, Globalisation and Corporate Nationalism: The New Cultural Economy of the New Zealand All Blacks*. Oxford: Peter Lang Publishers.
Scherer, J., & Jackson, S.J. (2013). *The Contested Terrain of the New Zealand All Blacks: Rugby, Commerce, and Cultural Politics in the Age of Globalisation*. Oxford: Peter Lang Publishers.
Sheard, K.G., & Dunning, E. (1973). The rugby football club as a type of male preserve: Some sociological notes. *International Review of Sport Sociology*, 8, 5–24.
Smith, B., & Sparkes, A.C. (eds.) (2016). *Routledge Handbook of Qualitative Research in Sport and Exercise*. London: Routledge.
Thompson, S. (1988). Challenging the hegemony: New Zealand's women's opposition to rugby and the reproduction of capitalist patriarchy. *International Review for the Sociology of Sport*, 23(2), 205–223.
Thompson, S. (1999). *Mother's Taxi: Sport and Women's Labor*. New York: SUNY Press.
Tracy, S.J. (2019). *Qualitative Research Methods: Collecting Evidence, Crafting Analysis, Communicating Impact*. New Jersey: John Wiley & Sons.
Trevett, C. (2016, September 13). Judith Collins and Paula Bennett to Chiefs: "grow up" and apologise. *New Zealand Herald*. www.nzherald.co.nz/sport/judith-collins-and-paula-bennett-to-chiefs-grow-up-and-apologise/C76URKNV4LZ3OUUC35LFKEF2VI/ [Accessed March 17, 2021].
Welch, M. (1997). Violence against women by professional football players: A gender analysis of hypermasculinity, positional status, narcissism, and entitlement. *Journal of Sport and Social Issues*, 21(4), 392–411.
Wenner, L.A., & Jackson, S. (2009). *Sport, Beer, and Gender in Promotional Culture: On the Dynamics of a Holy Trinity*. New York: Peter Lang.
Wright, J., & Clarke, G. (1999). Sport, the media and the construction of compulsory heterosexuality: A case study of women's rugby union. *International Review for the Sociology of Sport*, 34(3), 227–243.

9 Beer, promotional culture and women's rugby
Guinness' "Liberty Fields"

Sarah Gee

Many of the chapters in this book examine the historical evolution of the women's game as well as aspects and issues relevant to the lived experiences of female rugby players. These themes are essential as we consider how women's rugby has progressed from amateur play without coaches, team doctors or organised leagues to professional careers that include specific physiological and performance analyses and an advancement of the sporting subculture therein. Equally important are the ways in which large corporations use promotional culture and advertising to link their brands with women's sport, and with women's rugby in particular.

Advertising is a tool to symbolise and communicate ideologies (Goldman, 1992; Jhally, 2003), and "individuals depend on it for meaning – a source of social information embedded in commodities that mediate interpersonal relations and personal identity" (Harms & Kellner, 1991, p. 45). Sport-related advertising provides audiences with messages about gender identity and performance in sport, which in turn shape our personal ideas, beliefs and private experiences about what it means to be a male or female athlete. While some brands are beginning to showcase female athletes' and teams' athletic performances in their advertising (see Nike's "Dream Crazy" ad), specific examples of advertisements that feature, or relate to, women's rugby are scant. In the rugby context, beer companies are longstanding supporters of men's rugby (e.g., Heineken sponsors the Rugby World Cup and Steinlager sponsors the New Zealand All Blacks: see Gee, 2013; Gee et al., 2018). Promotional links between the alcohol industry and women's sport have been fairly limited until recently.

In 2019, beer brands Budweiser and Guinness both aired advertisements that served to position their brands as cultural advocates for significant social inequality issues related to women's sport. Women's sport is not only attracting more players but also calling for increased and equal pay, media coverage and sponsorship of elite female teams and leagues. Budweiser's social marketing efforts promoted its partnerships with both the US

National Women's Soccer League (NWSL) and the Canadian Professional Women's Hockey Players Association (PWHPA) and challenged both fans and other corporations to watch and support women's sport. Without doubt, there is a financial element involved in such partnerships. However, these types of campaigns publicly broadcast the attempts of alcohol brands to popularise their stewardship of such issues and become known as key activists to introduce change, make an impact on issues of inequality and grow women's sport. This is situated in a larger social, political and economic climate where equivalent forms of (financial) support from governments and other sport organisations are minimal or nonexistent.

This chapter offers a critical discussion of Guinness' "Liberty Fields" advertisement, which was released in the United Kingdom and Ireland in August 2019 ahead of the men's Rugby World Cup in Japan. The ad tells the story of the late 1980s Liberty Fields Rugby Football Club (RFC), a Japanese women's rugby team. The women formed their own rugby team after the Japanese Rugby Football Union refused to allow women to be associated with its organisation because the sport was considered too dangerous (Rausch, 2019). They represented Japan at the inaugural Women's Rugby World Cup in Wales in 1991. In the ad, women from the original Liberty Fields RFC speak of the stereotypical social struggles for women in Japanese society during the late 1980s and the cultural barriers they faced as women playing a physical, traditionally masculine sport. This chapter begins with an overview of the literature on rugby, gender, beer and promotional culture, which ultimately highlights how orthodox ways of understanding rugby and beer often include the notion that it "is not women's place" (Wenner, 2009, p. 124).

Rugby, gender and beer

The sport of rugby has a long association with drinking culture, hegemonic masculinity and alcohol sponsorship. Historically, rugby was an all-male preserve (Dunning, 1986; Nauright & Chandler, 1996), an exclusive male-dominated and male-defined space where men confirmed their masculinity through physical combat, the consumption of alcohol and, in some cases, the singing of songs that sexualised and objectified women. Even today, participation in rugby and its associated culture is among one of the surest ways to perform and conform to a dominant (or hegemonic) version of masculinity. It is argued that sport, more broadly, is one of the last frontiers of masculinity, given that it (1) provides the opportunity to perform sanctioned physical aggression; (2) provides a context for the demonstration of courage, commitment and sacrifice; (3) helps reaffirm historical links with war and the military; (4) offers an exclusive space for men away from work and family; (5) provides a context where groups of men can engage in regular body contact without the fear of being labelled gay; and (6) offers a legitimated, often corporate-sponsored, setting for the consumption of alcohol and, in particular, beer (Gee & Jackson, 2017). It is undeniable that beer and sport (and rugby in particular) are key signifiers of masculine identity. Wenner and Jackson (2009) conceptualise a sport, alcohol and masculinity nexus as a "holy trinity," and they highlight important concerns about how certain masculine sporting cultures, and the role of beer – as a highly masculinised product – within those cultures, impact the construction and negotiation of gender identities and relations.

Palmer and Toffoletti (2019, p. 109) contend that there is a need "to acknowledge that sport-related drinking for women is as pleasurable and problematic as it is for men," a concept currently understudied with respect to females. Although Carle and Nauright (1999) emphasise the importance of the consumption of alcohol as part of the overall culture of women's rugby, their discussion lacks significant weight to truly unpack it. More recently, Fuchs and Le Hénaff (2014) specifically examine the meanings that female rugby players associate with drinking during the after-match function or, as they label it, the "third halftime." Their findings indicate that female rugby players perceive drinking as a cultural norm to demonstrate their acceptance into the rugby culture of the club, but they recognise that the practice of drinking can also threaten how others view their performance of gender. Therefore, these women feel the need to participate in the expected drinking culture to maintain their "belongingness" to the group, yet they also need to simultaneously negotiate their entry into this traditional masculine domain without compromising their femininity. Fuchs and Le Hénaff (2014) conclude that the meaning of alcohol consumption for female rugby players is still linked to dominant social constructions of gender; however, it is interwoven with notions to preserve integrity and femininity.

Promotional culture, gender and beer

Beyond its purported, yet contentious, role in stimulating consumption, advertising plays an important ideological function not only with respect to the legitimation of capitalism and consumer culture but also within the politics of representation and identity formation (Jackson et al., 2005). There are a number of reasons for focusing on advertising as one of many aspects of promotional and media culture. Firstly, given advertising's centrality in relation to almost all constituents of contemporary media, it has been argued that the media have effectively colonised our culture (Goldman & Papson, 1996; Jhally, 1990). Secondly, the vast amounts of time, money and energy that are invested in making advertisements often exceed those of major Hollywood films, wherein the advertising industry increasingly secures the services of major film producers. In short, advertising is a major economic and cultural sphere in today's world. Thirdly, as multinational corporations continue to go global in search of new markets, advertising is frequently at the forefront of their strategies. Fourthly, advertisements, as cultural texts, provide material through which to understand our world (Jhally, 1997). In this regard, advertisements saturate our social landscape (Goldman & Papson, 1996), drive contemporary consumer culture, and not only influence patterns of consumption but also play an active role in identity formation within the context of late capitalism. For these and other reasons, advertisements serve as vital cultural artefacts for scholarly investigation.

Arguably, promotional culture is driven by the cultural economy of signs and signification (Goldman & Papson, 1996; Wernick, 1991) and represents and commodifies social identities (Cronin, 2000; Jackson, 2014; Nixon, 2003). Scott (2001) confirms the taken-for-granted social position of beer in society and alludes to the role that cultural industries, such as the media and advertising, play in setting the conditions and conventions around how we think about beer. In this vein, Strate (1992) suggests that beer advertisements "provide a clear and consistent image of the masculine role; in a sense, they constitute a guide for becoming a man, a rulebook for appropriate male behavior, in short, a manual on masculinity" (Strate, 1992, p. 78). Some scholars examine the sport-beer-masculinity "holy trinity" through critical textual discussions of advertisements and other media campaigns that serve to naturalise and safeguard this sacred relationship (see Gee & Jackson, 2012; Jackson, 2014; Wenner & Jackson, 2009). These narratives perpetuate strong connections between sport and men and between beer and men, and they strengthen the normalised practice of marketing beer brands through men's sport. Taken together, studies interrogating promotional culture in this way further articulate how "the social construction of masculinity is closely related to the cultural currency of beer" (Palmer, 2019, p. 281) and to sport.

This is not to ignore the notion that one significant cultural capacity of the advertising and promotional industries is that they continually monitor (and invent) trends and experiment with new strategies in pursuit of new markets for their clients (e.g., global brands). It is important to note that the advertising industry rarely has to make a choice between one market or another. In other words, it can afford to be inclusive and legitimate a greater range of gendered identities. While women have featured in beer commercials, they almost always occupy stereotypical, supportive roles as sex objects or cheerleaders. Women are rarely portrayed as actual consumers of beer. In this sense, there is a need to acknowledge that while the media produce cultural messages that frequently reflect gender stereotypes, they are also contested sites "where struggles over gender hegemony may create alternatives to restrictive polarised notions of masculinity and femininity" (Humberstone, 2001, p. 68). Yet, popular culture is largely devoid of beer commercials that challenge the notion of "emphasised femininity" (Connell, 1987) and feature strong and empowered females, let alone drawing connections to women's sport, especially one that is traditionally male-dominant such as rugby. This is because the link between beer, women and sport is not only unnatural it is nonexistent. Drinking beer is fundamentally masculine, and women's drinking is predominantly viewed as a transgression of gender-appropriate behaviour. As Killingsworth (2006, p. 357) argues, "in a wide range of cultures, alcohol is seemingly regarded as the stuff of men, not women, and drinking as a mark of masculinity, not femininity." Palmer (2015a) proposes that one reason for this unnatural association is directly attributed to scholars having theoretically and conceptually limited discussions about the relationship between sport, gender and alcohol because they use hegemonic masculinity as the prevailing framework. Palmer (2015b, p. 43) further suggests that "there are new relationships emerging between sport and alcohol, which also begin to question the dominance of hegemonic masculinity as a conceptual framework." These new relationships include a nascent research agenda on sport, alcohol and women (see Palmer & Toffoletti, 2019). In some respects, this chapter represents the humble beginnings to address the dearth of literature on women, sport and beer commercials; however, it is not specifically positioned in a postfeminist sensibility, as recommended by Palmer and Toffoletti (2019).

While alcohol advertising and sponsorship of women's sport have, to date, been fairly limited, female consumers have been recognised as a major target market by the alcohol industry (Taylor, 2017). Therefore, it is not surprising that women's sport will become an increasingly strategic vehicle for alcohol sponsorship. Women's rugby is not only attracting more players, in part due to the debut of rugby sevens at the 2016 Summer Olympics, but, similar to other sports codes, female rugby players are also calling for increased and equal pay, media coverage and sponsorship of elite teams and leagues. As previously mentioned, in 2019 two beer brands (Budweiser and Guinness) were key cultural trailblazers that used social marketing campaigns to increase public and corporate attention about issues of gender inequality in sport. For Guinness, 2019 marked the beginning of a six-year partnership with the Women's Six Nations rugby competition. Underscoring the significance of this new relationship and its potential to reach new audiences, former international rugby player Danielle Waterman states, "Recognition like this from big brands is key to help promote the importance and value of the women's game and also supports bringing it to new audiences" (Diageo, 2019). In August 2019, Guinness released its "Liberty Fields" minidocumentary, which is described in the next section.

The "Liberty Fields" minidocumentary[1]

As part of Guinness' long-standing "Made of More" campaign, the 5-minute "Liberty Fields" minidocumentary opens with a black screen, the Guinness logo and the word "Presents." Next is a series of quick-cut scenes of a close-up shot of an older Japanese woman's face, an empty stadium, an empty locker room, a rugby game and downtown Tokyo streets. Noriko Kishida, captain of the Liberty Fields team, reflects about life in Japan in 1989: "People labelled women who played rugby as vulgar." Yukiko Dazai, who played the position of flanker on the Liberty Fields team, states, "It was back in the day when getting harassed, sexually and otherwise, was a given. Men expected women to be young, pretty and willing to quit their jobs for marriage." Noriko Kishida, captain, continues, "At the time, the women's team weren't recognised as official. So, we founded our own organisation." Retro video footage from Liberty Fields RFC in 1989 is shown intermixed with narratives from other players, who discuss joining the team, their feelings when playing rugby and their claim that they were among the best in Japan. Then a female TV announcer declares, "The first ever Women's World Cup will be held in Britain this April. Japan will be competing too." Yukiko Dazai, flanker: "When we decided to play at the World Cup and started training, rugby became 90% of our lives." Miwako Murakami, wing: "As female rugby players, even when we were going to the World Cup, our bosses would say, 'What's the point?' 'Is that really necessary?'" Yukiko Dazai, flanker: "People would say the most horrible things. But I was proud of how hard I worked. At the office and on the field. So I refused to let their words get to me." Mitsuko Tanaka, lock: "I felt this strength sprouting inside of me, telling me that I couldn't lose the fight. It made me invincible, even in the toughest of times." The minidocumentary progresses to Liberty Fields' games at the 1991 World Cup and the women's experiences, including their realisation of the scale of competition at the global level. Miwako Murakami, wing: "We were hit with the fact that the rest of the world was playing at a completely different level." Noriko Kishida, captain: "But the fact that all these women in the world played rugby gave me courage." Staring out on the hallowed Tamagawa field, home ground for Liberty Fields, Noriko Kishida, captain, admits: "We lose if women can't play rugby. The reason why we've kept on going is because we don't want to lose. I wanted society to accept that women could love this kind of sport too . . . not just men." Keiko Kawaguchi, hooker: "When I had the ball, I would charge forward, as far as I could. If they had the ball, I would take them down no matter what. I never knew I had such strength within myself. It blew my mind." The ad finishes with a black screen and the words, "Liberty Fields RFC Pioneers of Women's Rugby," followed by a vintage photograph of the Liberty Fields team, which fades to black with the Guinness logo and "Made of More." The next section discusses three key tensions in considering the relationship between beer, promotional culture and women's rugby as represented by "Liberty Fields."

Discussion

Researchers have argued, to varying degrees, that advertising is a reflection of society (Schudson, 1993). As a cultural field (Jhally, 1997), beer advertising provides insights into the key stories, themes and values that are relevant within particular social contexts at specific points in time. The recognition and momentum that women's sport is currently achieving through financial sponsorships and multiplatform media exposure from big beer brands, such as Guinness, raise questions related to (1) the nature of the promotion around a women-sport-beer relationship, (2) the potential for a perceived (in)sincerity behind the use of feminist themes in beer promotional campaigns and (3) an increased diversification in the ways in which the sport-alcohol link remains socially prominent and culturally significant.

Regarding the first question, within the genre of beer commercials, "Liberty Fields" is unique because it depicts an exceptionally unusual subjectification of women in beer commercials. Historically, women are typically portrayed in traditional gendered ways, as either "babes" or "bitches" (Hellman et al., 2018). As babes they are the sexual objects of men's desires; as bitches they inhibit men's enjoyment of beer and their social escapism with mates (Wenner, 2013). The women in "Liberty Fields" counter this conventional storyline and, instead, are positioned as strong-willed, independent and tough; feminist narratives that are absent in beer advertising. The ad details some of the struggles these women had to overcome in regard to long-standing social barriers and gendered expectations for women in Japanese society in the late 1980s. "Liberty Fields" portrays these women as nonconformists to the heteronormative femininity of 1980s Japan and openly refers to notions of gender and male hegemony and patriarchy as the cultural roots of women's subordination. Male bosses are depicted as cultural control agents who seek to negatively impact the women's motivation and empowerment in and through rugby. As a result, the women acted on feelings of risk, choice and self-enterprise to experience freedom, self-expression and friendship, all of which were important considerations of citizenship in an increasingly neoliberal Japanese economy in the late 1980s and early 1990s (Ong, 2006). Although "Liberty Fields" is a true story, it is a bizarre and unorthodox female-centric marketing strategy for a traditionally male-oriented brand (Guinness), product (stout beer) and practices (beer drinking and rugby).

Following on from this, it is also important to consider another key initiative that was occurring concurrently in Ireland. In recent years, the Federation of Irish Sport initiated a movement, entitled 20×20, with the purpose of changing the cultural perception of women's sport in Ireland (Federation of Irish Sport, n.d.). As such, 20×20 was a society-wide campaign aimed at increasing media coverage of women's sport, female participation in all levels of sport and attendance at women's games and events, all by 20% by the year 2020. For the week of August 21, 2019, the Federation of Irish Sport awarded the International 20×20 Sportswoman of the Week award to the Liberty Fields team and highlighted that "Guinness is heavily involved not alone with rugby in Ireland but also as title sponsors of both the Men's and Women's Six Nations Championships" (Federation of Irish Sport, 2019). The unknown, however, is whether the value of the Guinness sponsorship deals for the Men's and Women's Six Nations tournaments was equal. This highlights some concerns around brands being promoted as advocates for change in gender equality and their promotional messages that appear to seduce consumers to buy into their actions. However, a lack of complete transparency can lead the public to question the motives behind corporate involvement and investment in women's sport and to question whether their advocacy is evidenced in "equal" terms.

Secondly, and building on the first question, there is an overall upsurge of advertisements that are created with a female empowerment message, known in marketing terms as femvertising: "advertising that employs a pro-female talent, messages, and imagery to empower women and girls" (SheKnows Media, quoted in Drake, 2017, p. 594). Research examining the effectiveness of femvertising encourages marketers to use empowerment themes and suggests that it has a positive influence on brand attitudes, purchase intentions and emotional connections to brands (e.g., Drake, 2017). This sentiment is reflective of the conceptualisation by Goldman et al. (1991) of "commodity feminism." Windels et al. (2020) describe commodity feminism as the use of "liberation, empowerment, control, independence, or self-definition as a signifier for the brand" (Windels et al., 2020, p. 26). These themes are explicitly apparent in "Liberty Fields" and serve to link these messages with the Guinness brand.

The director of "Liberty Fields," Eliot Rausch, confesses his hesitation to create advertising campaigns that portray brands as bandwagoners on social issues and cautions against a promotional strategy that identifies and exploits particular vulnerabilities:

> I've been hesitant the last couple of years with brands virtue signalling, jumping on some kind of fringe or marginalised group . . . at first I was like, "are they jumping on a feminist train to check a box?" So I was hesitant but then I realised it was much more than that. I was compelled with the rebellion of conformity but not for the sake of individuation or autonomy or self-expression as much as it was finding community and I thought that was really unique.
>
> (Little Black Book, 2019)

These very sentiments suggest that advertising creators and producers recognise the importance of linking "brands to powerful symbols, and they see feminism as a fertile ground for finding new symbolic ideas for their advertising campaigns" (Windels et al., 2020, p. 30). "Liberty Fields" is evidence that beer brands are beginning to adopt themes of feminism to promote their brand, which is a strategy that a range of other brands have already employed (e.g., Nike; see Gee, 2019). As such, consumption is positioned as the answer to achieve empowerment and equality (Goldman et al., 1991; Windels et al., 2020). However, some researchers caution against using feminist ideals without a need to also question whether these types of advertisements truly change existing social injustices and structural inequalities (Gill, 2017). Does "Liberty Fields" draw on the notions of feminism to create a message that is depoliticised (Goldman et al., 1991)? A simple answer is yes. A more protracted response would criticise the brand for not denouncing the patriarchal culture of rugby boards or initiating other forms of political action to ensure gender equality in rugby. To do so would implicate the brand itself (and the broader beer industry), which is founded on the principles of patriarchal culture, and the brand's long association with men's rugby, an all-male preserve (Dunning, 1986; Nauright & Chandler, 1996).

Thirdly, Guinness claims to be a brand that is striving to represent greater diversity and reflect a new, more inclusive Ireland. At the launch of "Liberty Fields," former Irish international rugby player and current Chair of Sport Ireland's Women in Sport committee, Lynne Cantwell, commented,

> Women's sport has made significant strides in recent years. It has become much more visible yet plenty of barriers remain not just in terms of getting women involved and staying involved, but also perception. The story of "Liberty Fields" . . . shines a welcome spotlight not just on the obstacles to be overcome but the many benefits society

stands to gain from overcoming them and creating a more inclusive and diverse culture in sport and beyond.

(Irish Rugby, 2019)

Themes of inclusivity and diversity were also apparent in the responses from several others. According to Niall McKee, head of Guinness Stout Europe, Guinness seeks to strategically position itself on a national and global scale with links to a changing Irish society, including its legalisation of marriage equality. McKee asserts,

> The brand is having to work out how it makes a shift from really traditional masculine Irish brand . . . there's a new Ireland and we need to work out how we stand for that new Ireland which is inclusive, which is diverse, and which is a really exciting place.
>
> (Ashton, 2019)

A critique of these claims returns to the argument of alcohol consumption as an unhealthy practice and a global public health concern. Until now, beer commercials featured men as a range of characters between "losers" (e.g., Messner & Montez de Oca, 2005) and "real men" (e.g., Gee & Jackson, 2012), but perhaps most significantly as part of a sacred "holy trinity" with sport (Wenner & Jackson, 2009). Diversification of the themes in beer commercials extends the problematic association of sport with alcohol beyond the confines of men's sport and male consumers to women's sport and female consumers.

Conclusion

This chapter explored an example of promotional culture that is one of the first commercialised links between beer, women and sport. Scholars in the areas of sport marketing and promotional culture, sociology of sport, gender studies, sport communication and other related disciplines are encouraged to continue to build an evidence-based foundation that espouses this emerging research agenda. "Liberty Fields" uses narratives from female Japanese rugby players to tell their story of defying the social conventions of gender in Japanese society during the late 1980s and early 1990s by choosing to participate in rugby. Pressures to conform to men's expectations of gender stereotypes for these women as "young, pretty and willing to quit their jobs for marriage" and the belief that "getting harassed, sexually or otherwise, was a given" are heartbreaking, but not unimaginable considering the recent #MeToo movement, which was experienced as equally intensely in the UK and Ireland as in other more publicised locations. While the discussion in this chapter is not formally framed within a lens of postfeminist sensibility, "Liberty Fields" signals "the promotion of women as agentic subjects" (Palmer & Toffoletti, 2019, p. 112) and signifies "popular cultural forms of postfeminism that champion women's equality through demonstrations of personal empowerment, which include women 'owning' their femininity and exhibiting choice, agency and the capacity to succeed in all aspects of life" (Palmer & Toffoletti, 2019, pp. 111–112). Through "Liberty Fields," Guinness strives to be a brand that consumers perceive as understanding the importance of, and embracing, diversity and inclusion. The fact that it has taken 30 years for someone (or something) to (re)present this story reflects the changing nature of the cultural conditions that shape how women are represented (Toffoletti, 2016) –cultural conditions that have prevented and controlled the sharing of these and similar stories.

Note

1 Readers should note that there was also a shortened, 60-second advertisement produced that featured the same theme but less spoken narrative.

References

Ashton, I. (2019). How Guinness smashed stereotypes in women's rugby and beyond. *Creative Brief.* www.creativebrief.com/bite/how-guinness-smashed-stereotypes-womens-rugby-and-beyond [Accessed March 13, 2020].

Carle, A., & Nauright, J. (1999). Crossing the line: Women playing rugby union. In T.J.L. Chandler & J. Nauright (eds.), *Making the Rugby World: Race, Gender, Commerce.* London: Frank Cass, pp. 128–148.

Connell, R.W. (1987). *Gender and Power: Society, the Person and Sexual Politics.* Cambridge, UK: Polity Press.

Cronin, A. (2000). *Advertising and Consumer Citizenship: Gender, Images and Rights.* London: Routledge.

Diageo (2019). *Guinness Champions the Women's Six Nations.* www.diageo.com/en/news-and-media/features/guinness-champions-the-women-s-six-nations/ [Accessed March 13, 2020].

Drake, V. (2017). The impact of female empowerment in advertising (femvertising). *Journal of Research in Marketing,* 7(3), 593–599.

Dunning, E. (1986). Sport as a male preserve: Notes on the social sources of masculine identity and its transformations. *Theory, Culture & Society,* 3(1), 79–90.

Federation of Irish Sport (2019). *International 20×20 Sportswoman of the Week.* www.irishsport.ie/international-20x20-sportswoman-of-the-week-4/ [Accessed March 12, 2020].

Federation of Irish Sport (n.d.). *About 20X20.* https://20x20.ie/about/ [Accessed March 12, 2020].

Fuchs, J., & Le Hénaff, Y. (2014). Alcohol consumption among women rugby players in France: Uses of the "third half-time." *International Review for the Sociology of Sport*, 49(3–4), 367–381.
Gee, S. (2013). The culture of alcohol sponsorship during the 2011 Rugby World Cup: An (auto)ethnographic and (con)textual analysis. *Sport in Society*, 16(7), 912–930.
Gee, S. (2019). Advertising, sports, and gender. In J. Maguire, M. Falcous, & K. Liston (eds.), *The Business and Culture of Sports: Society, Politics, Economy, Environment*. Farmington Hills, MI: Palgrave Macmillan, pp. 257–272.
Gee, S., & Jackson, S.J. (2012). Leisure corporations, beer brand culture, and the crisis of masculinity: The Speight's "Southern Man" advertising campaign. *Leisure Studies*, 31(1), 83–102.
Gee, S., & Jackson, S.J. (2017). *Sport, Promotional Culture, and the Contemporary Crisis of Masculinity*. London: Palgrave Macmillan.
Gee, S., Thompson, A., & Batty, R. (2018). Rules of engagement: Sport sponsorship, anti-ambush marketing legislation, and alcohol images during the 2011 Rugby World Cup. *Journal of Global Sport Management*, 3(3), 266–283.
Gill, R. (2017). The affective, cultural, and psychic life of postfeminism: A postfeminist sensibility 10 years on. *European Journal of Cultural Studies*, 20(6), 606–626.
Goldman, R. (1992). *Reading Ads Socially*. London: Routledge.
Goldman, R., Heath, D., & Smith, S.L. (1991). Commodity feminism. *Critical Studies in Mass Communication*, 8(3), 333–351.
Goldman, R., & Papson, S. (1996). *Sign Wars: The Cultured Landscape of Advertising*. New York: The Gilford Press.
Harms, J., & Kellner, D. (1991). Critical theory and advertising. *Current Perspectives in Social Theory*, 11, 41–67.
Hellman, M., Katainen, A., & Seppänen, J. (2018). Gendered citizen constructs in beer commercials as a metatext of alcohol control policies. *Contemporary Drug Problems*, 45(2), 163–176.
Humberstone, B. (2001). Femininity, masculinity and difference: What's wrong with a sarong? In A. Laker (ed.), *The Sociology of Sport and Physical Education*. London: Routledge, pp. 58–78.
Irish Rugby (2019). *Guinness Launch New 'Made Of More' Rugby Campaign*. www.irishrugby.ie/2019/08/15/guinness-launch-new-made-of-more-rugby-campaign-2/ [Accessed March 13, 2020].
Jackson, S.J. (2014). Globalisation, corporate nationalism and masculinity in Canada: Sport, Molson beer advertising and consumer citizenship. *Sport in Society*, 17(7), 901–916.
Jackson, S.J., Andrews, D.L., & Scherer, J. (2005). Introduction: The contemporary landscape of sport advertising. In S.J. Jackson & D.L. Andrews (eds.), *Sport, Culture and Advertising: Identities, Commodities and the Politics of Representation*. New York: Routledge, pp. 1–23.
Jhally, S. (1990). *The Codes of Advertising: Fetishism and the Political Economy of Meaning in Consumer Society*. London: Routledge.
Jhally, S. (1997). *Advertising and the End of the World*. Northampton, MA: Media Education Foundation.

Jhally, S. (2003). Image-based culture: Advertising and popular culture. In G. Dines & J.M. Humez (eds.), *Gender, Race and Class in Media: A Text-Reader*, 2nd ed. Thousand Oaks, CA: Sage, pp. 248–257.

Killingsworth, B. (2006). 'Drinking stories' from a playgroup: Alcohol in the lives of middle-class mothers in Australia. *Ethnography*, 7(3), 357–384.

Little Black Book (2019). *Your Shot: Liberty Fields Forever*. https://lbbonline.com/news/your-shot-liberty-fields-forever/ [Accessed March 13, 2020].

Messner, M.A., & Montez de Oca, J. (2005). The male consumer as loser: Beer and liquor ads in mega sports media events. *Signs: Journal of Women in Culture and Society*, 30(3), 1879–1909.

Nauright, J., & Chandler, T. (1996). *Making Men: Rugby and Masculine Identity*. London: Frank Cass.

Nixon, S. (2003). *Advertising Cultures*. London: Sage.

Ong, A. (2006). *Neoliberalism as Exception: Mutations in Citizenship and Sovereignty*. Durham: Duke University Press.

Palmer, C. (2015a). Drinking like a guy? Women and sport-related drinking. *Journal of Gender Studies*, 24(5), 483–495.

Palmer, C. (2015b). *Rethinking Drinking and Sport: New Approaches to Sport and Alcohol*. Farnham: Ashgate.

Palmer, C. (2019). Sports, beer, and promotional culture. In J. Maguire, M. Falcous, & K. Liston (eds.), *The Business and Culture of Sports: Society, Politics, Economy, Environment*. Farmington Hills, MI: Palgrave Macmillan, pp. 273–283.

Palmer, C., & Toffoletti, K. (2019). Sport, alcohol and women: An emerging research agenda. *Journal of Australian Studies*, 43(1), 103–117.

Rausch, E. (2019). *Guinness Liberty Fields*. https://vimeo.com/353921636 [Accessed March 12, 2020].

Schudson, M. (1993). *Advertising, the Uneasy Persuasion: Its Dubious Impact on American Society*. London: Routledge.

Scott, B. (2001). Beer. In R. Maxwell (ed.), *Culture Works*. Minneapolis: University of Minnesota Press, pp. 60–82.

Strate, L. (1992). Beer commercials: A manual on masculinity. In S. Craig (ed.), *Men, Masculinity and the Media*. London: Sage, pp. 78–92.

Taylor, K. (2017, March 13). Beer giants have lost big by ignoring women – now they're trying to win them back. *Business Insider*. www.businessinsider.com/beer-giants-reach-out-to-female-shoppers-2017-3 [Accessed March 13, 2020].

Toffoletti, K. (2016). Analyzing media representations of sportswomen – expanding the conceptual boundaries using a postfeminist sensibility. *Sociology of Sport Journal*, 33(3), 199–207.

Wenner, L.A. (2009). Brewing consumption: Sports dirt, mythic masculinity, and the ethos of beer commercials. In L.A. Wenner & S.J. Jackson (eds.), *Sport, Beer, and Gender: Promotional Culture and Contemporary Social Life*. New York: Peter Lang, pp. 121–142.

Wenner, L.A. (2013). The media sport interpellation: Gender, fanship, and consumer culture. *Sociology of Sport Journal*, 30, 83–103.

Wenner, L.A., & Jackson, S.J. (2009). *Sport, Beer, and Gender: Promotional Culture and Contemporary Social Life*. Zurich: Peter Lang.

Wernick, A. (1991). *Promotional Culture: Advertising, Ideology and Symbolic Expression*. London: Sage.

Windels, K., Champlin, S., Shelton, S., Sterbenk, Y., & Poteet, M. (2020). Selling feminism: How female empowerment campaigns employ postfeminist discourses. *Journal of Advertising*, 49, 18–33.

Index

Note: Page locators in *italics* indicate a figure and page numbers in **bold** indicate a table on the corresponding page.

advertising: beer brands and women's sports 116–117, 119–120, 122, 124; brands and women's sports 116; campaigns 123, 124; femvertising 123
All Black, South Africa 101
American football 4, 15, 16, 19, 22
association football (soccer) 4, 7, 9–10

Bannier, Annie 11
barrette: banned 11; feminised rugby 9, 10
Beaver, Travis 31
Birch, John 5
Blalock, Jane 21
Bordia, Prashant 83
Branco, Braluio Henrigue 70
Brawley, Lawrence R. 75
Budweiser 116, 120

Camey, Suzi 70
Canadian Professional Women's Hockey Players Association (PWHPA) 117
Cardiff Arms Park 8, 9
Carle, Allison 118
Carron, Albert 75, 83
Castaing, Michael 93
Caudwell, Jayne 32
Chang, Artemis 83
Chase, Laura 13
Collins, Tony 5, 6
commodity feminism 123

COVID-19 pandemic 19
cumulative shared selections (CSS): analysis of stats 62, *63*, 64, *65*, 66–67; team performance impact 60–62, 67–68–70
Curtin, Jennifer 7

Dawson, Victoria 5, 6
Dazai, Yukiko 121

Eley, Maria 9

Federation of Irish Sport 123–124
Femina Sport, women's sport club 9
femininity: challenging social conventions 35; cisgendered 28; heterosexual 30–32; middle-class norms, early 8; preservation of 118, 120, 122, 126; whiteness of 39
feminism 18, 123, 124
Ferrasse, Albert 93
Fields, Sarah 13
First World War 8, 12
Football Association (FA) 10
Football Club Auscitain 91
Forlani, Audrey 96
Franchini, Emerson 70
French Association of Women's Rugby (AFRF) 11
French national rugby 59, 76
French Rugby Federation (FFR) 10, 93, 99n3

Fuchs, Julian 118
Fuchs, Marek 23

gender inequality 39, 120
Global Positioning System (GPS) 45
Good Friday game of 1876 7, 12
Great Split of 1895 6
Great War, the 8, 9; *see also* First World War
Guinness 116, 120–123, 125–126

Harvin, Al 21
heterosexism 28, 30, 33
Heuzé, Jean-Phillippi 83
Houdré, Marie 9
HSBC World Rugby Women's Sevens Series 19, 61
Hull 6, 12

International Ladies' Professional Rugby and Hockey League 16
International Rugby Football Board (IRFB) 18

Japanese Rugby Football Union 117
judo 70, 93, 96

Kawaguchi, Keiko 121
Killingsworth, Ben 120
Kishida, Noriko 121
Kvam, Paul 70

Lamb, Kevin 70
Le Hénaff, Yannick 118
Le Monde 93, 99n1
Leo Marcos, Francisco Miguel 83
lesbian 32
Liberty Fields (Guinness) 121
Liberty Fields Rugby Football Club (RFC) 117, 121–122
Longman, Jere 23

"Made of More" campaign 121–122
Markov process for performance evaluation 61, 69–70
masculine: activity, perceived as 4–5, 8, 13, 94, 117–118; hegemonic culture 32, 93, 104, 110, 117, 120, 122
McKee, Niall 125

Men's Rugby World Cup 117
menstrual cycle, effects of 46–47, 54–55
#MeToo movement 125
Miarka, Bianca 70
misogyny 28
Murakami, Miwako 121
muscle fatigue, less common in women 46

National Collegiate Athletic Association (NCAA) 15–16, 18–20, 24, 25, 70
National Federation of State High School Associations (NFHS) 18
National Intercollegiate Rugby Association (NIRA) 18, 20
National Provincial Championship (NPC) 103, 106, 108, 111
National Small College Rugby Organization (NSCRO) 18–19
National Women's Soccer League (NWSL) 117
Nauright, John 118
Newport Ladies 9
New South Wales Rugby League 10
New York Times 16–17, 21–23
New Zealand Rugby (NZR) 101–102, 112–113
Nicholas, Ceri 70

Palmer, Catherine 118, 120
performance: collective efficiency 59–60, 67, 70, 75; evaluating physical demands of 3, 47, **47**, 48; physical/physiological inequalities 46, 54–55; preventing injuries 46, 50–54, *52*, *53*; support services increasing 45; team analysis 62, 66–68, 69–70
Piscione, Julien 85
Portland Press Herald 21
Portland Women's Rugby Football Club (Portland WRFC) 16–17
postfeminism 126
Premier Club 103

queer 32, 39

Rausch, Eliot 123
repetition of high-intensity effort (RHIE) 48–49

Index

Respect and Responsibility Review (RRR) 101, 112–113
Ride, Sally 17
rugby: amateur 6, 51, 85, 91, 94, 98, 116; contact sport 10, 21, 23, 59–60; culture of 15, 93–94, 102–103, 104–107; data collection 61; elite female players 75, 116; gender and beer 117–120; gender bias 3–4, 9–12, 28–29, 39; gender order 3, 8, 12, 104, 112; injuries 36–37; institution and values 22, 104, 110–113; male behavior 119; male-female interaction 12–13, 32, 91, 95, 104, 108, 111; male presence, predominantly 3–4, 6–8, 9–10, 15, 19, 29, 120, 123; massacre game, defined as 97; players, female 6, 9, 22, 51, 95, 99, 102, 105, 118; scandals 101, 112; sexual (gender) stereotypes 102, 106, 120, 125; tackling the opponent 29, 33–38, 97; trainer, a coach's perspective 95–97; in the United States (*see* USA Rugby); village, rural areas 91, 94–95, 98; whiteness, gender violence and 28–29; women's, history of 16–17, 29; *see also* whiteness
rugby sevens: high intensity sport 48–49, 68; injury prevention 51, *52*, 54; injury rate surveillance 49; injury risk factors 50–51; international competition and performance 60–61, 64, 69; player performance 59–60, 68; players, collective performance 59–60, 67, 70, 75; playing time 67–68; registered women, globally 45; team performance 59–60, 62, 66–70; women's performance studies needed 61
rugby union: cohesion, task and social 74–75, 76–78, **78**, **79**, 79–82, 83–84; football 3–4, 7, 11; forwards and backs 75, 76; gender-segregated 9; history 3; performance, team 60, 74; players 46, 48–49, 55, 96, 99n4
Ryle, Gilbert 92

Saouter, Anne 94
scrumhalf 38, 79
Senior Club 103
sexism 28–30, 39, 93
sexuality 29–32, 102
Shirley, Kenneth 70
Smith, Aaron 101
social network analysis (SNA) 69
Sokol, Joel S. 70
Strate, Lance 119
Stripper-gate 101, 111

tackle: injury, aversion to 35, 38–39; one-on-one 33, 34; open-field 35; satisfaction from 34, 95
Tanaka, Mitsuko 121
Theuriet, André 9
Thompson, Edward 70
Title IX 19–20, 22
Toffoletti, Kim 118, 120
Toilet-gate 101, 111

USA Rugby: college participation fuels growth 19–21, 24–25; early struggles of 15–16; gender/racial bias 23, 29–30, 31; history of 16–18; media silence/misinformation 22, 24

Valentine, Emily 4–6, 8, 12
Valley News 20–21
Vecchio, Fabricio 70
violence: objective 28–29, 33, 36, 39; subjective 28, 29, 30

WAGS (wives and girlfriends/groupies) 102
Wallace, William 23
Weebe, Nita 6–7, 12
whiteness: benefit of, women's rugby 30–32, 39; challenges femininity 39; violence, seen as affinity for 35–36, 38–39
Widmeyer, W.N. 75
Williams, Jean 8
Williams, Serena 36
Women's Premier League 19
Women's Rugby World Cup 15, 18
Women's Six Nations Championship 75, 123
World Rugby 12, 45, 49
World Rugby Festival for Women (RugbyFest) 18

Yakima Herald-Republic 21
Yamazaki, Moï 71

For Product Safety Concerns and Information please contact our EU representative GPSR@taylorandfrancis.com
Taylor & Francis Verlag GmbH, Kaufingerstraße 24, 80331 München, Germany

www.ingramcontent.com/pod-product-compliance
Lightning Source LLC
Chambersburg PA
CBHW070552170426
43201CB00012B/1814